𝕮𝖔𝖑𝖚𝖒𝖇𝖎𝖆 𝖀𝖓𝖎𝖛𝖊𝖗𝖘𝖎𝖙𝖞

STUDIES IN COMPARATIVE LITERATURE

THE INFLUENCE OF MOLIÈRE
ON RESTORATION COMEDY

THE INFLUENCE OF MOLIÈRE
ON
RESTORATION COMEDY

BY

DUDLEY HOWE MILES

1971

OCTAGON BOOKS
New York

Reprinted 1971

by special arrangement with Columbia University Press

OCTAGON BOOKS
A Division of Farrar, Straus & Giroux, Inc.
19 Union Square West
New York, N. Y. 10003

Library of Congress Catalog Card Number: 71-159247

ISBN-0-374-95652-9

Printed in U.S.A. by
NOBLE OFFSET PRINTERS, INC.
NEW YORK 3, N. Y.

TO

THE MEMORY OF

MY MOTHER

PREFACE

THIS essay in comparative literature attempts to determine the nature and extent of the influence exerted by Molière on English comedy from 1660 to 1700. Its purpose is not so much to identify particular cases of indebtedness to the French master as to study the general features of his influence on the art and outlook of the period. I shall be gratified if it contributes in any way to a better understanding of Restoration comedy, or to a more extended appreciation of the greatest comic genius of France.

The book in its present form is the outcome of a series of studies of individual writers, begun some years ago at the University of Chicago and carried out in an effort to approach the scientific accuracy and thoroughness for which Dr. J. M. Manly is so well known. I have therefore examined nearly every Restoration comedy that was accessible to me. The results, indicated in the appendix, represent my personal opinion after careful deliberation over doubtful points. Those who have preceded me in the field have relied so largely on second-hand information or have been so much carried away by the desire of establishing indebtedness that a searching personal investigation was prerequisite to any safe generalizations. I do not pretend to have discovered every trace of influence in the period, but I think so few direct borrowings have escaped me that my results are a basis for valid induction.

In mechanical details the volume conforms to the series in which it appears. I have tried to make quotations exact, but without reproducing peculiarities in the use of italics, small capitals, and similar matters. Full titles to all references in the notes will be found in the bibliography.

In the preparation of the work I have contracted many obligations: to Professor Myra Reynolds of the University of Chicago for starting me on the subject; to Dr. J. M. Manly for generous advice and criticism; to Mr. A. E. Hill of the English Library of the University of Chicago, to Mrs. Margaret McKennon, Librarian of Southwestern University, to the librarians and attendants of Har-

vard College Library, to the officials of the
Library of Columbia University, for securing
or providing the necessary material; to Mr. H.
C. Chatfield-Taylor, who at one point in my
research cordially extended me the use of his
great Molière collection. Miss Winifred Smith
has generously assisted me in several matters.
In the Columbia faculty I am indebted to
Professor Brander Matthews for many helpful
suggestions and for criticism on points of importance, and to Professor J. E. Spingarn for
discussion of features of the treatment. It is a
pleasure to acknowledge also the very valuable
criticism of Professor Ashley H. Thorndike.
My chief obligation is to Professor Jefferson
B. Fletcher, through whose kindness it has
been possible for the volume to appear in its
present form, and for whose unfailing interest
I cannot here sufficiently express my gratitude.

COLUMBIA UNIVERSITY, June 1, 1910.

CONTENTS

THE INFLUENCE OF MOLIÈRE
ON RESTORATION COMEDY

CHAPTER I

MOLIÈRE'S COMEDY

IF on the street we see a man of pompous gravity slip upon a banana skin and sit down in a very abrupt and foolish fashion, we turn away to hide our amusement. If at the play we see a miser talking and gesticulating excitedly about his treasure to the secret lover of his daughter, the frightened lover replying each time with a reference to the daughter, we cannot keep from laughing at their mutual mistake. We know these incidents are comic, just as we know after a single reading that Shelley's *To a Skylark* is poetic. But when we undertake to frame a definition of the comic in general, we find success as difficult as our laughter has been irresistible. We may lose from sight whole groups of comic incidents and evolve some fine-spun theory that gives delight to a scholastic mind but seems incomplete to one with a keen zest for the comic in life and literature; or we may in the end content ourselves with the simple conclusion that the vast majority of comic effects depend upon the sudden perception of some incongruity or contrast not felt as serious or irreconcilable.

Advancing this statement of the case as a convenient summary rather than a bullet-proof definition, I may add that the comic is not an unvarying quantity, that the comic sense has on the contrary developed only in society, since it involves some norm or standard of comparison. I am stating a mere truism to say that man has arrived at his notions of the usual and the sensible only through contact with his fellows, and that the comic accordingly varies in different ages of the world and in different communities of the same age. Imagine a Hottentot or an inhabitant of the South Sea Islands suddenly transported to the streets of New York. He might laugh at the tall silk hats or the finely tailored suits, but those about him would be so far from joining in his laughter that they would smile at *his* bare head and scanty garments. Imagine how dismal a reception even the best hits in the most popular comedy, except those depending on the mere shock of surprise, would secure from a theater full of such men. For it is obvious that every comic effect in a play depends for success on the existence of a common viewpoint among the members of the audience, and that those events and persons in clearest contradiction with the manners and views of the audience will seem most comic. It follows from these remarks that the comic does not appeal to our sympathies. We may view with generous indignation the bent figure of Shylock leaving the court-room or shake our sides at the rollicking humor of Falstaff, but in the second case as truly as in the first the pleasure cannot properly be called an effect of the comic. In other words, the humorous differs from the comic, strictly so-called, in being consonant with warm affection. Comedy as a type in literature makes use of both kinds of appeal, but the introduction of humor is a development of modern times.

Related to this consideration of particular comic moments in a play is a difference between tragedy and comedy as subdivisions of the drama. Tragedy moves in an ideal world where the crimes and grand passions of men absorb our attention from the trivial and the commonplace. It neglects the superficial circumstance of life to pierce to the essential qualities of the soul in serious or irreconcilable conflict with universal law. This characteristic tendency is observable not only in Sophocles and Racine and Shakspere, but in such powerful moderns as Ibsen and Hauptmann and Echegaray. Comedy, on the other hand, has usually moved near the world of external fact, where the incongruities are more tangible and where they do not affect the issues of life too profoundly. It has accordingly depicted the common vices and ridiculous follies of mankind by means of types more or less easily recognized in the different countries where it has originated. Among the poets of the New Comedy in Greece so closely did Menander copy the details of the rich and polished society in which he lived that an Alexandrian grammarian exclaimed, "O Menander and life! which of you copied the other!" Whenever a poet of medieval England wished to relieve the somber tone of a miracle play with the brighter colors of comedy, he took some picture from shepherd life or went back through his experience to find a suitable shrew for Noah's wife. In France a long succession of farces copied matter from political and social circles so strikingly that at length Henry IV had to restrict subjects to private life. The *commedia dell' arte* of Italy, among many a synonym for conventionality in character drawing, was so realistic in its origin that several of the types appearing later in an unending series of masks are easily traced to separate localities in the peninsula.[1] The Spanish comedy of cloak and sword, which to foreigners seems a tissue of the most artificial imbroglios, was in the hands of Lope de Vega a not very much distorted reflection of the manners of the country. Indeed, it has generally been true that, regarded as types of drama, tragedy has tended to the ideal and the universal, while comedy has tended toward the realistic

[1] Cf. Moland, p. 12 ff.; Flamini, p. 313 ff.

and the local, because tragedy deals with
essential qualities and irreconcilable con-
flicts, while comedy deals with the incongruities of life, and succeeds only where the
norms of judgment prevalent in a community
are readily applicable.

Such closeness to the facts of life is characteristic of Molière, whom most Frenchmen
regard as the Shakspere of their nation. He
never mixes with his satire the boundless
fancy of Aristophanes or the charmingly
delicate creations of *A Midsummer Night's
Dream.* His interest is in life and the characters which everyday life presents. Such
interest, indeed, was peculiarly fostered by
the circumstances of his career. Born[1] in
the home of a prosperous furniture dealer
in a bourgeois section of Paris, he must have
seen more than one wealthy neighbor running
up long bills in a ridiculous effort to become
a "gentleman" in spite of many remon-
strances from his sensible wife. He may
have found in his own father[2] an example of
the unscrupulous money-lender who exacts

[1] Jan. 15, 1622.
[2] Cf. Larroumet, p. 15.

twenty-five per cent for useless old furniture
and hangings. Certainly the bourgeois attitude, with its common sense and spirit of
ridicule, was familiar to his childhood and
helped to mold the ideals of his boyhood
while he was a day student at the Collège de
Clermont. Later, when he had organized
a company of players and began his twelve
years of strolling through the provinces, he
enlarged his view of man to include every
variety of local type with its peculiarities of
costume and speech — simple peasant girls
and rascally servants ; pretentious country
aristocrats, unfortunate husbands, and thick-
witted suitors ; the bailiffs and collectors of
petty taxes, with all the self-important village
society aping the fashions of the metropolis.
On his return to Paris in his thirty-seventh
year and the establishment of his company
at the court of Louis XIV, he not only re-
newed acquaintance with the shopkeepers
of his father's quarter, but found new fields
for the penetrating observation of character
— listened to empty-headed courtiers and
prudish women of fashion, dined among the
devotees of a literary fad and the foppish

leaders of different court circles. His own troupe, too, and his family, gave him the most intimate understanding of the various turns that love and jealousy and other primary instincts of humanity take in men and women of different temperaments. Hardly could one imagine a career better suited to develop a full understanding of the essential unity of human nature and a keen sense of its manifold irregularities.

No one certainly has made more of his opportunities than Molière. He did not merely observe narrowly the superficial side of life, note the style of a coat or the color of a ribbon; he pierced below to the nature of the man. His friend Boileau summed up his character accurately in the word "Contemplator." The tradition which pictures him sitting in a provincial barber-shop, intent upon the frequenters conversing about business or gossip, is true in spirit if not in fact. The other picture which one of his enemies has preserved is as illuminating as it is vivid. In one scene of the comedy *Zélinde* a character describes what he saw Molière doing in the shop below: "Élomire didn't utter a word

all the time I was down there. I found him
leaning on a counter like a man who was
dreaming. He kept his eyes glued on three
or four ladies of quality who were haggling
over some lace. He seemed to listen intently
to what they were saying, and from the
movement of his eyes you would have said
he was piercing to the bottom of their souls
to discover what they were secretly thinking.
I even believe he had a note-book and that
under his cloak he took down unperceived
the best things they said. He's a dangerous
man. There are some people who take their
hands everywhere they go. You might say
of him that everywhere he goes he takes his
eyes and ears." [1]

This absorbing interest in character as it
manifests itself in everyday life is a distinguishing feature of those comedies which he
produced in rapid succession during the
fifteen years that intervened between his
return to Paris and his death.[2] For this
reason the classification of his work is diffi-

[1] A translation of *Zélinde*, sc. 5, quoted in Molière,
Œuvres, x. 279.
[2] Feb. 17, 1673.

cult; serious objections can be brought to almost any grouping of his plays. The first two, *L'Étourdi* and *Le Dépit Amoureux*, written and first performed in the provinces, very clearly belong to the comedy of intrigue type, where the plot consists of a succession of improbable incidents and confusing complications, the characters little more than marionettes pulled hither and yon at the need of the artificial situations, the interest centered in the ceaseless movement and the constant surprise furnished by the turning and winding of the plot. Yet in *L'Étourdi* Eraste is no more of a mask figure than the hero of *Le Menteur*, a piece formerly acclaimed as the beginning of comedy of character; and in *Le Dépit Amoureux* the love quarrel is presented with so much naturalness that it could be acted to day as a scene in any modern comedy. *Les Fourberies de Scapin*, brought out at the height of Molière's career, is also a brilliant specimen of the *genre*. But in others, such as *Monsieur de Pourceaugnac* and *Le Médecin malgré lui*, the satiric treatment of manners takes up so much of the play and exercises so controlling an influence on the structure

that one hesitates to put them in this class.
Such uncertainty, however, does not obscure
the fact that one group of Molière's plays,
larger or smaller according to the precon-
ceptions of the classifier, may be called comedy
of intrigue.

Another group may be styled romantic or
heroic-pastoral: *Don Garcie, Mélicerte, Les
Amants Magnifiques, Le Princesse d'Élide,
Psyché, Le Sicilien*. Except the first, which
was an effort of Molière to win fame as a
serious poet, they were produced to furnish
entertainment at the royal *fêtes* of Louis XIV,
and were interspersed with ballets, in which
the king and his courtiers delighted to appear.
Though many passages display a poetic grace
in the treatment of ideal persons and places
not usually attributed to this champion of
common sense, these plays, with the exception
of the pleasing trifle, *Le Sicilien*, contain little
evidence of Molière's comic powers or his
genius for observation. The group may
therefore be neglected in a study of his influence on Restoration comedy.

The type of comedy which belongs distinctively to Molière and upon which his

greatness as a dramatist is based falls entirely under the head, comedy of manners and character. The beginning was made in *Les Précieuses Ridicules*, the action of which is in the tone of farce. But the action is not what holds our attention; it is only a frame for the picture of an affectation in the actual life of the day. Molière virtually took typical figures from the parterre, set them on the stage, and thus allowed the audience to watch itself. In *Sganarelle* the incidents are likewise chosen to render ridiculous the typically absurd jealous husband, but the interest of the audience is centered on the irresistibly laughable series of *qui-pro-quo* situations, so that the piece is comedy of intrigue instead of comedy of manners. But with *L'École des Maris* and *L'École des Femmes* Molière became clearly conscious of his aims. He forsook conventional types and artificial imbroglios, so far as his public would allow, in order to express his own convictions about the society around him which he knew so well. Sometimes he was obliged to modify his design to conform his play to the whims of the *Grand Monarque* who was his patron, as one sees clearly in the

last acts of *Le Bourgeois Gentilhomme;* sometimes he developed his idea into no more than
a sketch, an excuse for the ballets which were
all the go at court, as in *La Comtesse d'Escarbagnas;* sometimes he mingled an element
of farce with the satire of mankind, as in
L'Avare; but everywhere he displayed his
absorbing interest in actual life and living
characters. In two of his plays he dealt with
subjects of such profound and universal significance that by some they have been termed
comedies of character *par excellence,* and by
others high comedy, as a kind of comedy
rivaling tragedy in the importance of the
interests involved. Certainly these two, *Le
Tartuffe* and *Le Misanthrope,* with a third,
Les Femmes Savantes, reveal the essential
qualities of Molière in the chief comic masterpieces of French drama.

Indeed, one may go further and say that
the beginning of French comedy of manners
is to be found in this third class of Molière's
work. The great mass of comedy produced
in the period before Molière's advent was
totally different in spirit. The old French
farce and its realistic satire of political, social,

and private life had disappeared from the theater before the universal popularity of the *commedia dell' arte*, with its conventional types of character and artificial plots. In higher kinds of comedy the same spirit prevailed. Larivey in the last quarter of the sixteenth century had done much to establish the Italian tradition, to center interest on intrigue instead of on manners, to deal with equivoke and disguise, the turns of chance and deceit, instead of imitating nature. This intrigue type was revived in the second quarter of the seventeenth century by Rotrou, who delved in the inexhaustible mine of Spanish comedy for a vast variety of unreal situations. He was followed by Scarron, who took almost every one of his plays from Spain, burlesquing his sources by an enormous buffoonery and an exaggerated satire that made the theater echo with laughter. This same cleverness in devising variations and combinations of incident in a world subject to few of the conditions of actual life was continued by Thomas Corneille even after the close of Molière's career.

These general statements concerning the

predecessors of Molière are, like all general
statements, subject to exceptions. In *La
Belle Plaideuse* of Boisrobert we look into a
shop in the jewelers' section of Paris and see
the mingled crowd of high society and *bourgeoisie*. The picture is superficial, but it is
copied from life. In *Les Visionnaires* of
Desmarets a succession of almost unconnected
scenes presents a succession of "humors" in
something of Ben Jonson's manner, with the
purpose of interesting the audience in the
faithfulness of the delineation. The great
Corneille also made some advance toward
a comedy of manners. In *La Galerie du
Palais* we overhear the talk of linen-drapers
and woolen merchants, booksellers and book-
buyers, quite different from the artificial
language of contemporary plays. We see
also an actual servant instead of the tradi-
tional nurse. *Le Menteur* is likewise a beginning for true comedy, improbable as the hero
is ; for some scenes, such as that between
Dorante and his indignant father, are the
necessary result of character. But all these
plays are interesting chiefly as prophecies.
The incidents are still ingenious inventions,

not natural occurrences; the customs are still touched with artificiality; the characters are still mere sketches; the dialogue is not yet the conversation of men and women from the street, the shop, and the home, expressing their own ideas and feelings. In short, even these few forerunners of the coming change did not hold to the conception of allowing the audience to watch itself in typical characters moving about on the stage. This revolution in taste from the strange to the natural is what Molière's comedy of manners accomplished.

The reason why the innovation succeeded is that Molière is a typically French author. He has all the clearness and logic of the race. He indulges in no irresponsible imaginings. He gives way to no allurements of the fancy delighting in its own capriciousness. He presents instead some eminently reasonable Ariste or Cléante, who explains, often at a length that wearies English ears, what might otherwise seem nonsensical or wrongheaded. Chance does not determine the succession of events in his plays as it does frequently in the romantic comedy of Shakspere and Fletcher.

Even when his plot is brought to a close by the discovery of long-lost parents or the intervention of a powerful king, the *dénouement* does not impress one as illogical. Certainly one of his distinguishing traits is lucidity.

He also has the lightness of satire that belongs to the indefinable *esprit gaulois*, a hatred of the wearisome and the pedantic, an instinctive delight in ridicule and raillery without bitterness or rage, a laughter full of vivacity but arising from the keenest logic. The definition I gave a moment ago of the comic, "the perception of incongruity," is especially applicable to the French. They take little pleasure in the free play of the imagination for itself. Their laughter is always reasonable.

He was typically French, too, in putting meaning into his work. The plays which delight English readers, *A Midsummer Night's Dream* or *The Tempest*, are ill-understood by most Frenchmen. They seek to comprehend what ought to be enjoyed by the imagination. They feel insecure in the cloudlands of fancy. Their abiding sense of reality is troubled by these unsubstantial pageants that fade and pass away into nothingness. But in *L'École des Femmes* and *Les Femmes Savantes* they find the familiar circumstances of life arranged so as to present a penetrating view of marriage and woman with the utmost gaiety and clearness. Beneath the lightness of the French is this insistent seriousness of taste, which takes deep pleasure in what seems didactic and prosaic to Englishmen because its gaiety is not careless and unreflecting.

Another reason why Molière succeeded in effecting the change in taste from the extraordinary to the natural is that he wrote in the opening years of the reign of Louis XIV, when the French nation was most French.[1] It will be recalled that the successive approaches toward establishing the absolute power of the crown made by Louis XI and Henry IV were all but completed by Richelieu before his death in 1642. He robbed the magistrates of their powers, supplanted the princes and nobles by ministers of his own creation, and reduced the people to payers of taxes. During the ministry of his successor, the Italian Mazarin, the different elements,

[1] For this period, cf. Lavisse.

heartened by the Puritan successes in the
Civil War in England, rose for the last time
against this centralization of authority. This
series of disturbances, known as the Fronde,
was characterized by a spirit of faction. The
kingdom was distraught by shifting purposes
and enmities, — magistrates siding now with
the people and later timidly resigning themselves to the royal power ; a prince this day
leading the armies of France, the next fighting
against them with the revolutionists, later
entering the service of Spain ; the people
themselves barricading the streets of Paris
against the royal troops, driving the royal
family out of the palace, covering the streets
with satires on Mazarin and his foreign
associates, and later filling the *bourgeoisie*
with uncertainty and dread. Distrust and
fear were rife. Society was in a state of dis-
integration.

Moreover, the nation was not, and for some
time had not been, wholly French. Foreign
manners in dress and behavior were made to
prevail in higher circles under the influence
of Anne of Austria and the Hôtel de Rambouillet, but had not yet been assimilated to

the national character. The theater was so
thoroughly foreign that it is safe to say half
the successful plays were taken from Spain.
Even the lowest classes, no longer clamoring
for the old farce, stood wide-eyed before the
antics and improvisations of the Italian companies in the *commedia dell' arte.*

With the subsidence of the Fronde in the
middle fifties the nation came into its own.
The late disturbances had aroused among the
middle classes a keen desire for order and tran-
quillity, which the succession of Louis XIV in
1661 soon turned into patriotic exultation in a
king of their own race who governed with justice, revived languishing industries and com-
merce, and later made French arms victorious
wherever they appeared. The bourgeois of
Paris who ten years before had been afraid of
having his doors beaten in by gangs barricading the streets, now settled into a comforta-
ble, prosperous condition, self-satisfied and
self-regarding. Even in the late fifties the
banker, the lawyer, the merchant, instead of
scanning his neighbor suspiciously, began to
observe with lively interest the vices and follies developed by peaceful life. His standards

of conduct became more definite and universal under the growing culture of the age. The enthusiasm of the bourgeois was aroused by the splendor of the court to which Louis drew every noble of the realm by making all dependent on his exchequer. The mingling of noble and bourgeois encouraged by Louis's disregard of birth and artificial advantage in the distribution of responsibilities and rewards tended to supplant the peculiar prepossessions of the *bourgeoisie* with saner standards of judgment. More influential was the Hôtel de Rambouillet, with its introduction of the refining influence of woman on society and conversation, which had for many years helped to spread broadcast norms of conduct through the formation of many circles of imitators.[1] Men had become keen and quick-witted, impressionable to finer shades of distinction, and at the same time less individual and prejudiced in judging conduct and character. Thus political and social conditions combined to transform the rude audience of Richelieu's day into a polished worldly society with greater community of

[1] Cf. Livet.

feeling and taste than had ever existed before in France.

For it will be remembered that even by 1636 [1] the common people had ceased to attend theatrical performances. They thronged the mountebank's show by Pont Neuf or the fairs at Saint Germain, but the theater was filled with the higher classes, who, as has been shown, were becoming more and more refined and gradually developing a strong spirit of society, which is always hostile to individual variation from accepted usage. It was to this society, which had at length assimilated the elements of foreign culture and developed its own native traits, that Molière appealed. [2] He, a child of old Paris, reared, as I have related, in its traditions and familiar with its prejudices, voiced the spirit of its merchants and bankers when he laughed at the extravagances of the *précieuses ridicules*, the inflated ambition of Monsieur Jourdain, the foolish aspirations of Léonard de Pourceaugnac, the ridiculous pretensions of Comtesse d'Escarbagnas. But

[1] Cf. Reynier in Petit de Julleville, iv. 358 f.

[2] For a study of these audiences, cf. Despois, livres v., vi.

there is something more than the prepossessions of his class even in these plays, and
in *Le Misanthrope* he produced a drama it
would have been impossible to produce in
1660, a drama which is as perfect an expression
as the spirit of society has ever attained.

The uniqueness of Molière's comedy is not
explained by the circumstances of his life,
nor by his French characteristics — his clearness and logic, his instinctive satire and
seriousness of purpose — nor even by the
strong social tone that pervades his work.
All these features show how he could accomplish what was virtually a revolution in public
taste, but the peculiar quality of his work is
to be found after all only in his genius. It
is very difficult to give an adequate idea of
his *vis comica*, of the inexhaustible gaiety
which sets so many scenes ringing with silvery
laughter. Difficult as this comic spirit is to
define, he would be dull indeed who could resist
the dialogue of Sosie with his lantern in *Amphitryon*, or the lesson in philosophy given to Monsieur Jourdain, or the consultation of self-suffi-
cient Sganarelle with suspicious Géronte in *Le
Médecin malgré lui*. Literature contains few

figures so inextinguishably comic as the impertinent Dorine of *Le Tartuffe* or the archly malign Toinette of *Le Malade Imaginaire.* Even in his most serious situations his verve appears in hardly diminished vigor. When the headstrong miser is about to strike his obstinate son, the servant breaks in to relieve the strain with the unconscious buffoonery of his reconciliation. When the audience is oppressed by the impending doom of Orgon, the incredulous stepmother opens the door to brighten the whole scene with delightful comedy. When the jealousy of Alceste has become almost painfully intense, the breathless valet appears to draw forth volleys of laughter while he searches every pocket for the note he has forgotten to bring from his master's table. The gaiety which enlivened many a medieval fabliau and farce has nowhere found a more hearty or vivacious expression than in the comedy of Molière.

Let me repeat, however, that this *vis comica* is different in origin from that familiar to English readers in the work of Shakspere and Jonson. Molière has none of Shakspere's fantastic and ideal creations ; no mischievous

Puck or light-footed Ariel glides through his scenes. Nor is he much closer to the Shakspere who leaves the stage to those irrepressibly witty fools and clowns who engage in the lively give and take of conceits or entertain the spectator with a nice derangement of epitaphs. To the pit in Elizabethan days Feste and Launcelot Gobbo were humorous rather than purely comic figures ; that is, the audience laughed with them rather than at them. Both carman and courtier might have said with a ring of hearty good-nature, "How witty the fool is !" or "What irrepressible humor the clown has !" Molière presented figures decidedly different. He delineated a Monsieur Jourdain to point the folly of colossal conceit, or a servant Martine to show up the ridiculousness of affectation and pedantry. Ben Jonson is somewhat nearer to Molière's comic spirit. Yet even *The Alchemist*, generally considered Jonson's best performance, is not very much in the style of *Les Femmes Savantes*. In the handling of Dapper and Drugger and Sir Epicure Mammon we see all too clearly the Plautine conception of comedy, in which no emphasis is laid on the unsocial or insincere elements of character. The comic effect does not come so much from the absurd expectations of those characters as from the supremely witty way in which the expectations are defeated of fulfilment. The play is a contest of the clever with the dull or unsuspecting, and we laugh with those who get the better. The Plautine conception appears in Molière also, but it is modified by a conviction, more profound than appears anywhere in Jonson, even in *Bartholomew Fair*, that conduct should conform to the demands of society. In his comedy of manners he laughs at the attempt of folly and vice to supplant nature and reason. His gaiety arises from the feeling that the irregularities of ordinary life are in themselves irresistibly amusing.

But one who thinks only of the comic verve of Molière is far from understanding his attitude toward life. The universality of his appeal does not rest on the widespread desire of men to be diverted. Had that been the case, he would have been superseded in his own country by Regnard, Beaumarchais, and Scribe, and would have found small audience outside of France. He was not only an unrivaled comedian, but a thinker upon some of the profound problems of life. Yet he was not a philosopher with an ordered system. All his comedies rest upon very few convictions. He believed most thoroughly that our guide in life should be our own instincts. Whoever tries to suppress or distort the natural impulses becomes ridiculous. If Arnolphe rears a child in ignorance and restrains her from all the normal pleasures of youth, even his sufferings shall be made ridiculous. If Cathos and Madelon renounce the common language and customs of everyday life for the artificial jargon and manners of a romantic world, they shall be most humiliatingly deceived. In other words, Molière is one with the pagan spirits of the Italian Renaissance in their full reliance on the goodness of human nature and their disregard for the restraints of a religion which had undertaken to control every variety of human conduct. He too believes in the goodness of human nature, and goes on repeating in play after play: "Be natural. Follow your normal impulses. That is the rule of life."

This injunction carries with it the corollary, "Be sincere." It is only the man who distrusts or falsifies or despises nature who becomes hypocritical. Consequently Molière attacks every form of insincerity with relentless vigor. Physicians who pretend to assist the human body, which needs no assistance, who repeat empty terms handed down from the ancients without the slightest knowledge of the organism for which they prescribe, who profess to administer wonder-working remedies when their only purpose is to line their pockets with gold — all these hypocrisies of medicine he ridicules with never diminishing zest. But hypocrisy is sometimes too much even for the inextinguishable gaiety of Molière. Tartuffe, who forbids the innocent diversions of the young wife, who dries up the husband's sincere affection with the consuming breath of bigotry, who wishes to crush the tender love of the daughter and defeat the rightful expectations of the son, who would even seduce the wife of his benefactor, — this sinister figure is depicted, not in gay, but in somber colors, because he is the very antithesis of Molière's injunction: "Follow nature.   Be sincere."

Sincerity, however, may be carried too far. Alceste is passionately sincere, but he is ridiculous. One naturally asks why the man who embodies so many of Molière's own characteristics, his hatred of affectation and pretense and conceit, his hatred of double-dealing and hypocrisy, whose devotion to sincerity reflects one of the very strongest devotions of Molière's soul — why this man is nevertheless ridiculous. The answer is simple : because he forgets he is living in society, because he is unsocial. This Molière never forgets. The man who follows instinct must do so with the abiding consciousness that he is living among men, that his conduct must be subject to the rule of common sense and sound judgment. Thus Molière is after all vastly different from the pagan spirits of the Italian Renaissance. He believes in none of the immoderate enthusiasms of individualism, in none of the strange eccentricities of originality. Life must be subjected to order and reason. We must not demand of it the impossible, unless we wish to taste a bitterness like that of Alceste, almost as deep as the suffering of that Arnolphe who

tried to defeat nature for his own personal
ends.

Thus it comes about that Molière is something more than a comedian presenting
realistically the superficial and the local
incongruities of life so as to make their
contradiction with the norms of judgment
prevalent in his community readily apparent.
This typical Frenchman, with all the logical
clearness, spirit of ridicule, and underlying
seriousness of his race, this poet of the age
of Louis XIV, when the society for which
he wrote attained a greater unity than had
ever before existed, not only becomes the
greatest master of comedy in French drama
by the inextinguishable gaiety of his genius,
but also, by his profound insight into life
and the sweet reasonableness of his attitude
toward it, stands forth as one of the significant figures in the history of European
literature.

CHAPTER II

WHILE Molière and his compeers, La Fontaine and Boileau and Racine, were helping to produce that literature which shines forth as the peculiar pride of Frenchmen, there arose in England with the return of Charles II a literature of similar classical tendencies which Englishmen have consigned to a limbo of the half forgotten. Yet the period merits consideration, not only for the satire of Dryden, which every one knows something about, but for the dimly remembered drama which filled the theaters for the four decades following Charles II's return. It is of course true that nearly all the tragedy bears traces of Corneille and Racine from France and of Shakspere from among the Elizabethans, but a few of those tragedies have seldom or never been surpassed in all the succeeding two hundred years. The heroic play, moreover, sneer as much as we may at its extravagant language and impossible characters, challenges our attention because it awoke the enthusiasm of thousands of playgoers and absorbed much of the energy of the leading poet of the age. But the achievement of the Restoration was its comedy, an achievement which some critics have regarded as the most brilliant in English dramatic literature. To study this comedy will be the purpose of this and the following chapters.

Restoration comedy was not perfectly homogeneous. Though the different varieties will be seen later to have a great deal in common, lines of distinction can be drawn. There is first the old comedy of humors which had been developed by Ben Jonson, its plot consisting of a series of appropriate retributions for the variations from a norm which were represented by the different characters. It awoke to a faint life in the early work of Dryden and was galvanized into strange contortions by Ben's faithful disciple, Thomas Shadwell. Then the Spanish comedy of intrigue, with its constant appeal to the attention by a brisk succession of incidents, a form which had in English been foreshadowed by the prolific inventiveness of Fletcher, sprang for a time into promising popularity under the influence of King Charles, who was so fond of it that he suggested Spanish plots for some of the dramatists to imitate. Its vogue as a distinct species did not develop, but the intrigue plot, imported either directly from Spain or indirectly through the medium of Thomas Corneille or other French imitators of Calderon and the Spanish school, continued to form a large element in the comedy of the age. These types, however, are not what give to Restoration comedy its peculiar distinction. The type which was then developed to its greatest brilliancy belongs to the species that Molière cultivated — a comedy of manners which holds the mirror up to the follies and foibles of society without assuming the frown of a judge or uttering the jeer of a satirist. So conspicuously is this form the achievement of the period that Restoration comedy and comedy of manners have often been used as convertible terms.

There had indeed been in English drama an approach to comedy of manners before this date. Truly notable is the famous comedy of humors already mentioned. It is rightly considered the invention of Ben Jonson, not only because Chapman's *Humorous Day's Mirth* is hardly entitled to consideration in spite of the fact that in plot and treatment of character it is virtually an anticipation of *Every Man in his Humour*, but also because the immense development of the type and its long vogue were due to Jonson entirely. It presented the follies and affectations of contemporary life with a veracity that not even Wycherley excelled. Every playgoer was convinced of the reality of boastful Boabdil and of Sir Epicure Mammon. Even to-day we walk once more in old Saint Paul's with Fastidious Brisk, and laugh as heartily at the absurd mistakes of Zeal-of-the-Land Busy as if we ourselves were strolling through the side-shows of Bartholomew Fair. After Jonson left the stage, such plays as Cartwright's *The Ordinary* (1634), Marmion's *The Antiquary* (1636), and Jasper Mayne's *The City Match* (1639) maintained the type down to the closing of the theaters. It is hardly necessary to point out that the whole school was not so much interested in picturing contemporary manners as in drawing individual eccentricities of character. The writers touched upon the follies of everyday or fashionable life, but they satirized, not the social failing as such, but the personal deviation from a norm. They thus diverged from a true comedy of manners by centering their interest elsewhere than in the imitation of society.

Nearer to the type under discussion are those plays which reveal a genuine interest in scenes of everyday life for themselves. Not to go back to *Hick Scorner* or *Gammer Gurton's Needle*, every one remembers *The Two Angry Women of Abington* and Lamb's hearty praise of it.[1] *The Merry Devil of Edmonton* and *The Merry Wives of Windsor* also contain scenes from the village or rural circles of the time. A whole play of the type, its pictures of daily London life, tinged to be sure with a charming color of romance, is seen in Dekker's *Shoemaker's Holiday*. A breath of satire inspires *Eastward Hoe*, and a gross realism approaching the moral indifference of the Restoration weighs down two companion

[1] Cf. Lamb, *Works*, iv. 426.

pieces, *Northward Hoe* and *Westward Hoe*. In Middleton we find a dramatist devoting a good part of his time for a long period of years to the faithful reproduction of scenes from the actual London of his day, in a manner which was perhaps slightly influenced by the satiric intent of Jonson's humors and the romantic tendencies in plot of contemporary drama, but which in spirit approached very closely to the worldiness of Etheredge and Dryden.[1] Among the followers of Middleton, Field produced two comedies [2] which by the impudence of their amorous intrigue might have gained them a few representations at the court of Charles II,[3] but which show very clearly the influence of Jonson's gulls and roarers. The influence of Jonson is even larger in Brome's plays, in some of which the presentation of London life drops below Middleton or Field in the prosaic coarseness of the realism.

Besides this type of comedy of manners,

[1] For a study of Middleton as a writer of comedy, cf. Fischer.

[2] *A Woman is a Weathercock* and *Amends for Ladies*.

[3] *A Woman is a Weathercock* was, in fact, revived at Lincoln's Inn Fields in 1667. Cf. Genest, i. 79.

which was written mainly for the butcher
and the baker, there was another which had
in view more or less the courtier and the inns-
of-court man. This form was developed by
John Fletcher, who infused into the realistic
study of contemporary life a lightly ad-
venturous tone that made all men soldiers
of fortune, and who added to the charm of
such study by the spiciness of his characters
and the romantic daring of his plots.[1] Even
when the scene was London (as in *Wit without
Money* or *The Night Walker*) this romantic
element was prominent, and it generally became so controlling that the study of manners
was disguised under a foreign garb and the
English characters masqueraded as little
French lawyers or Spanish curates. Massinger's *Guardian* bears witness to the popularity
of this courtly type. Nearly the whole body
of Shirley's comedy likewise depicted the
higher grades of social life under one mask or
another, and with a cleverness of plotting
that was apparently also suggested by
Fletcher. In this class of plays the basic element in a comedy of manners, the imitation of

[1] Cf. Hatcher, *John Fletcher*, p. 35.

life in a fashionable circle more or less apart, is more prominent than in the preceding class, but in all the productions of the school the interest in reality is largely replaced by interest in incident and plot. With these qualifications, however, it is true that even before the closing of the theaters comedies of manners directed either to the mass of citizens or to the throng of courtiers had already formed a large body of dramatic literature.

It should nevertheless not be forgotten that this body of literature differs in several respects from the Restoration comedy of which the following chapters are a study. Not much stress need be laid on the general use of verse by the Jacobean writers and the almost universal use of prose by Restoration playwrights.[1] Comedy of manners in the earlier period tended to prose dialogue, many plays of Middleton and Brome having very few speeches in meter. But the dialogue of Middleton, in spite of the flashes of wit and satire, does not approach the brilliant repartee of Congreve, that realistic but polished imi-

---

[1] Crowne's *Married Beau* is the only exception outside of tragi-comedy I know of.

tation of what the society of Charles II's time regarded as the chief ornament of conversation.

Not much need be said concerning the handling of plot in the two periods. The school of Etheredge and Wycherley, in virtue of a closer approximation to the manners of its circle, is on the whole less extravagant in the violation of probability than the followers of Middleton and Fletcher. Nor is the combining of two or more stories in a single piece a distinguishing feature of the school. English popular playwrights had from the beginning sought to hold the attention of the audience by an abundance of action, even to the extent of joining plots that had no real connection. If many Restoration plays are a mere jumble of such unrelated plots, they are simply a few degrees worse than some productions even by the masters of pre-Restoration comedy. In the attitude toward unities other than that of action a striking difference may be noted. The frequent change of scene and the long lapses of time among the Jacobeans are a notable feature of the stage and plot-management.

Only two of Fletcher's comedies,[1] for instance, come within a limit of twenty-four hours, and many of them extend over a period of months or even a year. The constant change of place becomes at times almost kaleidoscopic, hurrying us hither and thither so as to give an impression of bustle and rush which any amount of action by itself would hardly produce. But the tendency through all Restoration comedy is to keep the scene in the same locality and to compress the time as much as possible to the limits of a day and night. This was in part due to the introduction of painted scenery.[2] But we shall see later that French discussion of the unities, and especially the models followed by the dramatists, were a much stronger influence in lessening the number of scenes and shortening the time of dramatic action.

A more fundamental difference between the two periods is the selection and treatment of subject-matter. The Restoration was given over almost entirely to picturing the manners of fashionable life ; even when influenced by

[1] *The Mad Lover* and *The Chances.*

[2] On this introduction, cf. Downes, pp. xx. f., xxiv. f., 20 f.; Wright, p. 412; Pepys, iii. 157 (June 13, 1663).

the comedy of intrigue it found its material largely in an imitation of the social customs of the times. The Jacobean comedy of manners in its different kinds down to the closing of the theaters was fundamentally either comedy of intrigue or comedy of humors, the transcript from contemporary life being introduced as of secondary importance and interest. Even such a realistic play as *A Trick to Catch the Old One* is essentially an intrigue-comedy, and *A Mad World* clearly employs Ben Jonson's plot-method. The truth is, the men who wrote comedies of London life had not yet reached the conception which the leading Restoration playwrights soon gained, that of centering the interest in a picture of contemporary manners. The poets like Middleton, who had a genuine interest in studying life realistically and satirizing various features of it, always felt it their first duty to keep up a busy action or to reveal new eccentricities of character. As a consequence of focusing its interest on social life, Restoration comedy placed much more of its action in interiors, within coffeehouses or boudoirs or reception halls, than in

fields or streets or perhaps the undesignated
rooms of a house. The development of
painted scenery merely added vividness to
this employment of local color. A second
consequence was that an amorous intrigue
formed the basis of nearly every Restoration
plot, since such intrigues were held to be the
chief recreation of the fashionable circles of
the day. Jacobean comedy, on the contrary,
in spite of its partial loss of the wholesome
atmosphere of the Elizabethan period, still
moved in ways relatively more modest and
wholesome. I am not unaware of the several pre-Restoration plays of London life
that dealt with adultery and kindred vices.
Any one who examines these latter will
find in them an important difference from
the attitude of Restoration writers. Leaving out of account a few anomalous productions like *The Parson's Wedding*, we find
that such writers as Field and Brome and
Shirley finally cleared those suspected of in-
fidelity. Whoever speaks of their plays as
rivaling the comedies of Charles II's court
forgets this very material consideration. The
Restoration audience delighted to see the

young gallant succeed; some pre-Restoration audiences apparently enjoyed risky situations, but they at the same time demanded that virtue triumph in the end.

The difference between the two ages in this matter is typical. The audiences of Jonson and the tribe of Ben had a healthy interest in frank realism; the audiences of Wycherley and Dryden were characterized by a cynical indifference to moral considerations. Nor can it be urged that Jonson is also indifferent to moral considerations. To be sure, *The Alchemist* and *Bartholomew Fair* cannot be called strictly moral, — the knaves generally get the better of the pious. Yet the knavery is of no base or disgusting nature, so that we for the moment agree that the victims are too dull to deserve a better end. The Restoration not only laughed at witty rogues but applauded the crimes of youth and pleasure. Every restraint was felt as an impertinence, and they who most ingeniously and successfully evaded those restraints became the most delightful figures in the theater. The explanation of this state of affairs is not far to seek. Imagination was dead. Men

were entirely absorbed in the hard or frivolous
facts of life. Chivalric ideals no longer
shaped their conduct, and they felt small
desire to escape from fact into any poetic
fairyland of the imagination. Self-sacrificing
love and knightly honor might exist in some
world of dreams, but for such men as Rochester and Buckingham dream-worlds had no
existence even in the sounding couplets of
an heroic play except as a subject for ridicule
and immoderate laughter. He who would
not be known for a fool had to look at the
world of material existence with the clear
eyes of common sense. Since virtue and
chivalry no longer molded men's thoughts
or influenced their actions, what could playwrights do but fashion the scenes about them
into a long succession of *Relapses* and *Plain
Dealers?* The age for Rosalinds or even
Sad Shepherdesses had given place to one of
Royal Academies and the tenacious recognition of fact.

This formula fits the whole school remark-
ably well. The different members, of course,
had individuality. After reading them carefully one comes to feel very marked personal

characteristics. But the class traits are more numerous and striking than in the Jacobean period. No one would think of confusing Middleton with Fletcher or Massinger with Shirley. Equally obvious would be the similarities between even Wycherley and Congreve. In the days of the first Charles, to be sure, there were many hack writers whose manners are scarcely distinguishable, but the prevailing effort to invent novel situations shows that originality was yet prized. Men strove not to be like each other and recognized no common standards toward which all should tend who sought perfection. In the Restoration originality found little place. It was an age of adaptors and imitators. Men no longer felt an impelling individual inspiration. The greatest writers borrowed incidents and characters for the most successful of their productions, and were following models in the most brilliant of their creations. They prided themselves on being members of a fashionable class, living their life apart from the body of the people. They recognized the integrity of a clique, and were guided constantly by the taste of their own small circle.

The rivals of Jonson and Fletcher had to take into account a more various audience. Here, indeed, lies the secret of nearly all the differences we have noted between the two periods.

The audience of the early Jacobean period is graphically described by Dekker in those satirical directions which he gave, in the chapter, "How a Gallant should behave himself in a Playhouse," to those boorish fellows of the day who wished to pose as gentlemen of fashion : —

Sithence then the place is so free in entertainment, allowing a stool as well to the farmer's son as to your templar ; that your stinkard has the self-same liberty to be there in his tobacco-fumes, which your sweet courtier hath ; and that your carman and tinker claim as strong a voice in their suffrage, and sit to give judgement on the play's life and death, as well as the proudest Momus among the tribe of critic : it is fit that he, whom the most tailors' bills do make room for, when he comes, should not be basely, like a viol, cased up in a corner.[1]

It is clear enough, then, that in 1609 the play-house attracted well-nigh every element of the population, that the audience was truly

[1] Dekker, p. 49 f.

representative of the national life. This condition accounts for the undeniably English tone even of those plays where the scene was laid in foreign lands or the characters were taken from a restricted part of the population. He who wrote of kings and dukes made as broad an appeal as he who presented only shoemakers and apprentices. The taste of the city and the taste of the court, though not identical, were by no means antagonistic or mutually exclusive.

Before the reign was out James had contrived by his theories concerning divine right and ecclesiastical authority to stir up more than ever the opposition of the Puritan party.[1] Its time-honored hatred of the theater was fed also by the magnificent spectacles which Ben Jonson and Inigo Jones were creating under royal favor. The gradual drawing away of the mass of the people from the playhouse found ample expression in the next reign in the *Histrio-mastix* of William Prynne. This valiant author declared with some bitterness: "that many, that any gracious, godly, growen, faithfull Christians, who are

[1] For this whole subject, cf. Thompson.

thorowly instructed in the wayes of godli-
nesse, or in the noxious qualities of Playes,
doe constantly, doe frequently resort to Playhouses, to Stage-playes, (especially out of
a loue or liking unto Playes themselves) I
utterly deny." [1] He further asseverated
"that they who resort to Playes and Playhouses, have not so much as the least Symp-
tomes of any Christianity in them ; that they
are worse then men, then beasts, then Devils." [2]
The over-zealous barrister had to admit, however, " that perchance some few exorbitant,
scandalous histrionicall, (but farre from good)
Divines" and "some puny new-converted
Christian Novices " " may sometimes visit
Theaters." [3] The proportion of good people
who did so was much larger than he was willing to concede.   Killigrew, says Pepys, "tells
me plainly that the City audience was [then]
as good as the Court." [2] This evidently
means that the respectable part of the city,
not merely the idle and frivolous or the low
and brutal, formed as large a part of the audience as the hangers-on at court.   He did

[1] Prynne, p. 151.   [2] *Ibid.*, p. 427.   [3] *Ibid.*, p. 150.
[2] Pepys, vi. 163 (Feb. 12, 1666–7).

not have in mind the Fortune and the Red
Bull, which were "mostly frequented by
citizens and the meaner sort of people," [1]
but the "private houses," the Blackfriars,
Cockpit, and Salisbury Court, which "had
pits for the gentry." [2]   For Wright, speaking
evidently of the reign of Charles I, declares
that very good people then thought "a play
an innocent diversion for an idle hour or
two." [3]   We must therefore conclude that
down to the close of the elder drama the writers
took into account various elements of the
population, that the city itself continuod to
furnish whole audiences, and that the taste
of the court was tempered by that of the
middle classes. The success of a play still
depended upon the breadth of its appeal.

There can of course be no doubt that in the
England of the fourth decade the audiences
were less representative of the whole nation
than those described by Dekker at the close
of the first decade. The *Memoirs of Colonel
Hutchinson* for the later period reveal how
wide had become the separation between the
court and the serious, self-respecting element

[1] Wright, p. 407.   [2] *Ibid.*, p. 408.   [3] *Ibid.*, p. 407.

of the population.[1] The drama itself furnishes abundant evidence. The later plays
of London life, unlike those produced in the
early years of the century, which were leveled
more or less at the taste of shoemakers and
apprentices without losing the strong interest
of all grades of society from prince to pauper,
were in several cases apparently written for
the frequenters of the tavern and the gaming
table. Such, I imagine, were a great many of
the comedies presented at the Fortune or the
Red Bull.[2] Scarcely more representative of
the body of the people was the great mass of
drama, beginning with Fletcher, which sought
primarily to interest the languid courtiers
who had developed a somewhat fastidious
taste through the performance of masks and
pageants. The taste even of the average
playgoer from among the gentry was headed
in Charles I's time toward the taste of the
Restoration; he delighted in the gulling of
a would-be gallant from the country or the
humiliation of a puritanic citizen. But it
is important to remember in this connection

[1] Cf. Hutchinson, i. *passim*, especially p. 114 f.
[2] Cf. Fleay, pp. 358 ff., 363.

that he was still far from demanding what
the playgoer of Charles II's time demanded.
Fletcher had continued to draw common
characters sympathetically,[1] and his plays
were still popular. Shirley, to be sure, was
more distinctly a court poet, in one piece
entering into collaboration with the King.
His plays were of course presented at the
private houses. He, however, is an extreme
illustration of the tendency. Massinger
surely wrote for men as sturdily English as
any who applauded Middleton or Dekker,
yet his pieces were presented at those same
Drury Lane or Blackfriars audiences. Besides, the traditions of the great period were
ever before the poets of the later decades, as
one can see in the most courtly of them
all, Shirley himself. The atmosphere of the
clique, the consciousness of appealing to a
narrow circle only, was thus prevented from
becoming oppressive. The theater was no
longer a truly national pastime, it is true,
but the drama as a whole retained in various
degrees an unmistakably English tone and
a corresponding breadth of appeal.

[1] *E.g.*, Gillian in *The Chances*, Syphax in *The Mad Lover*.

The Restoration audiences were more homogeneous. The manager Killigrew told Pepys the City had almost ceased to appear at the theater.[1] Wright at a later date (1699) corroborates him with the statement that "the playhouses are so extremely pestered with vizard-masks and their trade (occasioning continual quarrels and abuses), that many of the more civilized part of the town are uneasy in the company, and shun the theatre as they would a house of scandal."[2] A single glance from the stage will show how great the change was from pre-Restoration times.[3] We see the upper gallery chiefly occupied by the footmen[4] of the lords and ladies who sit in the pit (or parquet) and the boxes below. Women of loose character throng into the middle gallery[5] and crowd even into the prominent places in the pit among the ladies of quality. The latter appear also in the circle of boxes which runs

[1] Cf. Pepys, vi. 163 (Feb. 12, 1666-7).

[2] *Op. cit.*, p. 407.

[3] Cf. Lowe, *Thomas Betterton*, chap. iii.

[4] Cf. Dryden, *Works*, x. 399 f.

[5] *Ibid.*, p. 399; Congreve, epilogue to *The Double Dealer*.

around the pit under the galleries. The chief
resort of the wits and all the leaders of the
day is the pit itself. Thither they repair,
often as early as shortly after noon, the house
sometimes being filled by one o'clock.[1] The
elegant idlers pass the time pleasantly enough
chaffing the orange girls [2] or conversing with
the vizard-masks, not stopping when the play
begins if the damsel prove witty enough, even
though, as in Pepys's case, other spectators
by that means lose the pleasure of the play
wholly. [3] Yet it was the opinion of such
beaux in feather and flaxen periwig that determined the success or failure of the comedy.
They remained after the performance to discuss its merits and "decree the poor play's
fate," [4] for, their judgment once known, "all
the town pronounces it their thought." [5]
Hence the fops and wits were the determin-
ing element in these Restoration audiences ;
it was for them the playwrights wrote, and
it was by them the humbler members of the

[1] Cf. Pepys, viii. 223 (Feb. 25, 1668–9).

[2] Cf. Vincent, *Young Gallant's Academy* (in Dekker,
p. 105).

[3] Cf. Pepys, vi. 176 (Feb. 18, 1666–7).

[4] Dryden, *Works*, iii. 97.   [5] *Ibid.*

audience were convinced. For the "citizens, 'prentices, and others" who at one performance seemed to Pepys "a mighty company" in the pit and a sign of "the vanity and prodigality of the age," [1] were certainly the admirers and would-be imitators of the rakes of the court whose escapades had given the tone to society.

Nothing can be more striking than the unity of these audiences, than the absorbing interest manifested in the sayings and doings of the leaders. The office clerks whom Pepys mentions,[2] we must believe, took as vivid an interest in the King's mistress and were as much pleased to fill their eyes with her as the worthy Clerk of the Acts himself,[3] and they were possibly as much troubled at a later performance to see Lady Castlemain look dejectedly and slighted by people already.[4] Nor can their delight at the coarse repartee of those notorious actresses, Nell Gwyn and Beck Marshall, have been less than his.[5]

---

[1] Pepys, vii. 244 f. (Jan. 1, 1667–8).

[2] Cf. *Ibid.*, i. 307 (Jan. 19, 1660–1).

[3] Cf. *Ibid.*, ii. 64 (July 23, 1661).

[4] Cf. *Ibid.*, p. 225 (May 21, 1662).

[5] Cf. *Ibid.*, vii. 161 (Oct. 26, 1667).

It is possible that some of the citizens who frequented the playhouse had their hair pulled by a vizard-mask less distinguished than Mrs. Knipp,[1] and thus began in imitation of Rochester or Buckingham an affair which occasioned more than one quarrel with their wives.[2]

For it should be remembered that the leaders of these audiences led outside the theater impudently dissolute lives. It would be a grievous error to repeat the frequent assumption that the whole body of society was permeated by the moral rottenness of the court. The more idle and frivolous or weak-kneed and self-indulgent gave way to the license of the times, but the great mass of the sturdy, self-respecting middle class that had supported the Puritan movement of the preceding decades did not suddenly forsake their bourgeois virtues and strong moral prepossessions. They simply held themselves in retirement and kept away from the theater altogether. Moreover, even the many vacillating spirits who fell in with the playgoers and

---

[1] Cf. Pepys, p. 62 (Aug. 12, 1667).
[2] Cf. *Ibid.*, viii. 233 (May 4, 1668).

were caught in the tidal wave of reaction from the Puritan *régime* boasted of a defiance they were far from putting into practice. After these reservations are made, the picture of society is one of the darkest in the modern history of England, especially in the first decade, when the reaction was most violent, but also, in a diminishing degree, down to the publication of Collier's *Short View*, when the middle-class ideals once more gained control. We know from various sources that the gallants who directed courtly taste in theatrical matters spent a good part of their time in seeking diversions, in running from theater to theater or sauntering through Hyde Park till they found some interesting damsel or till all the fine ladies had taken their leave ; they visited the crowded shops of the New Exchange, took journeys to Epsom Wells, or conducted themselves with such shameless impudence toward women that it troubled Pepys "to see the confidence and vice of the age." [1]   The theater itself was one of the chief centers of such immorality ; the career of Nell Gwyn was typical of the stage life of the

[1] Pepys, viii. 67 (July 27, 1668).

period.[1] So general was this looseness of life at the beginning of the period that King Charles, when he wished to convene Parliament on short notice, sent to the theaters and houses of ill-fame to summon the members to meeting.[2] How could it be otherwise when Charles himself set the example,[3] "squandering on his mistresses the £70,000 voted by the House for a monument to his father"?[4]

With such audiences dominated by such leaders the playwrights could not do otherwise than produce a drama far different from the unmistakably English drama of pre-Restoration times. Instead of appealing to men from virtually every class in the nation, they depended for success on the suffrage of a narrow court circle led by the most dissolute rakes of the day. The tendency of comedy to develop new characteristics in this new social *milieu* was strengthened by the prevailing French taste of the court circle.[5]

[1] Cf. Cunningham, *Story of Nell Gwyn*; Pepys, vii. 19 (July 13, 1667).

[2] Cf. Pepys, vi. 88 (Dec. 8, 1666).

[3] Cf. *Ibid.*, vii. 259 f. (Jan. 11, 1667–8).

[4] Cunningham, p. 104.

[5] For this whole subject, cf. Charlanne.

The royalists who had followed Queen Henriette to Saint Germain or who later fled to the Continent before Cromwell, enjoyed for many years the balls, concerts, promenades, and various *fêtes* provided for their entertainment at Fontainebleau or in the vicinity of the Louvre. Although these cavaliers were very glad to return to England for the favors which they felt Charles II would shower upon them, they returned with a genuine liking for the French manner of living and thinking. They were still haunted by the charms of the superior civilization of France. Fashions in dress during the whole Restoration period were adapted more or less from French styles, — hats and periwigs, gloves, mirrors, perfumes, ribbons, and rings were brought from Paris with lace, embroidery, and fans. Even carpets, coaches, and clocks had to be imported with the wines from Bordeaux and the cheese from Calais. In short, French taste was the mark of good society. He who could not converse in French lacked one of the essentials of good breeding. Nothing could be more natural than this revolt among men who held in detestation the severe simplicity of the Puritan *régime* and wished to get as far away as possible from the ascetic ideal of dress and conduct.

This spirit of reaction, furthered by a genuine liking for French taste, was in the drama tempered by the force of no strong national literary tradition. The cavaliers themselves knew almost nothing of the glories of the elder drama, and the few writers like Killigrew and Davenant who survived from pre-Restoration times were totally incapable of repeating the Jacobean achievements or even of continuing the work of Massinger or Shirley. During the first ten years, to be sure, the revivals of plays by the school of Fletcher and Jonson were constant, but the courtiers felt like Pepys that these things were hardly to their taste. The King himself, who was especially interested in the theater, at one time commanding Lacy to act in the place of Clun [1] and frequently ending disputes in the theatrical companies by his command or decision,[2] at once took upon himself the substitution of new models. To Tuke

[1] Cf. Pepys, iii. 108 (May 8, 1663).
[2] Cf. Cibber, i. 89.

he suggested a Spanish plot for *The Adventures of Five Hours*. The author, who remarks that his majesty's "judgment is no more to be doubted than his commands to be disobeyed," [1] declares that the Spanish are the happiest nation in the world "in the force and delicacy of their inventions." [2] The King's interest in the Spanish drama did not wane, for not long before his death he pointed out to Crowne *No Pued Esser* for the intrigue of *Sir Courtly Nice*.[3] But it was not the models from Spain which were to determine the trend of Restoration comedy. That trend was to be determined by two young writers who had spent their youth and formed their taste in France. They were to develop a new species of English comedy by introducing Molière to English audiences.

[1] Dodsley, xv. 194.
[2] *Ibid.*
[3] Cf. Crowne, *Works*, iii. 254, 245 ff.

CHAPTER III

THE two men who introduced the influence of Molière into Restoration comedy were Sir George Etheredge and William Wycherley. Etheredge was one of the most elegant wits of his time. Not very much is positively known of his life, but it is certain that he was one of the gay band of cavaliers who drank in the delights of Saint Germain with Prince Charles. How deep a draught he took may be inferred from his plays, which show that he knew all the fashionable shops and was familiar with the peculiar customs and usual topics of conversation in the *beau monde*.[1] The Parisian experience must have been enjoyed by this indolent pleasure-lover, who nevertheless took a keen interest in observing the amusements of others. On his return to

[1] *E.g.*, cf. *Love in a Tub*, iii. 4 (p. 51 ff.); *Sir Fopling Flutter*, iii. 2 (p. 296 ff.); *Ibid.*, iv. 2 (p. 338 f.).

61

London some three years after the Restoration,[1] he joined the circle of men about town, spent this afternoon in the coffee-house, sauntered that evening about the paths of Mulberry Garden, sat the next day in the pit at Drury Lane to hear Mohun in *The Humorous Lieutenant* or at Lincoln's Inn Fields to witness Dryden's *The Wild Gallant*. But these plays must have seemed to him lacking in vitality — they were not close enough to his ordinary life to arouse much enthusiasm. "I can do better than that myself," he must have thought to himself, remembering the triumph Molière had achieved in *Les Précieuses Ridicules* by transcribing a Parisian fad. He accordingly set to work and in 1664 produced *Love in a Tub*.[2]

Such I conjecture to have been the origin of Etheredge's first comedy. He certainly had been profoundly impressed by *Les Précieuses Ridicules*, as we shall find in *Sir Fopling Flutter*. But at the moment he saw nothing in London corresponding to the French

[1] Cf. Meindl, p. 9 f. ; Gosse, *Seventeenth Century Studies*, p. 235.

[2] On the date of production, cf. Pepys, iv. 304 (Jan. 4, 1664–5).

farce, so that he presented a picture of the roystering circle in which he moved and filled out the play with a serious action in heroic couplet One thread of the comic plot, the attempts of Palmer and Wheedle to swindle Cully, is an intrigue of Jonsonian comedy placed in a Restoration setting. But the central feature of the plot, the courting of the widow by Sir Frederick and of her maid by his valet Dufoy, harks back to Molière. The suggestion for the action was found in the fortunes of Éraste and his servant Gros-René in *Le Dépit Amoureux*, but no more than the suggestion. The idea of introducing a subplot dealing with maid and servant he borrowed, but the characters and incidents were all taken directly from his own experience of London life. Dufoy is one of the French valets whom the cavaliers had brought across the Channel on their return to England. Sir Frederick is a young blood whose amusements are waging a bloody war with the constable, "committing a general massacre on the glass-windows," and knocking at a lady's lodgings at two o'clock in the morning as if he were upon a matter of life and death. It was this reproduction of the world of gallants and dandies which made the play more successful than any Davenant's company had produced, bringing to the actors a thousand pounds in the course of a month.[1]

In this appeal to recognition, not in the suggestion for a part of the plot, lies the real influence of Molière in the play. How important the influence was for the period may be surmised from the statement that *Love in a Tub* was the first Restoration comedy to center the interest in the recognition of one's acquaintances and pastimes in the figures and scenes on the stage. *The Wild Gallant* had indeed contained a dim reflection of the yet unformed society of the realm, but the persons were worked up as humors supposed to be interesting for their eccentricities, and the customs were described in a purely incidental fashion. Etheredge did the new thing of presenting typical figures which were interesting because they were typical. His attitude toward the life he copied was thus like Molière's detachment, but he went beyond Molière to a position of almost com-

[1] Cf. Downes, p. 25.

plete indifference. He not only refused to take sides with or against his characters, but he did not hold them up to any standard of sound sense or social welfare.

The immense success of his first production made Etheredge a favorite with the wits of the courtly circle. This is probably one of the reasons why he worked out his second play more carefully. *She Would if She Could* (1668) at any rate marks an advance in dramatic construction, for the plot is unmixed with tragedy and the threads are skilfully interwoven. It also marks an exclusiveness in the point of view which may be traced in part to Etheredge's greater intimacy with the leaders of fashion. The main plot, in all likelihood suggested by a frequent incident of London life, is the pursuit of a town gallant by a country lady aping town manners. The idea implies not only a change in the dramatist, but a development of unity in the worldly society, a consciousness of its own ideals and of its separateness, which cannot be paralleled in earlier Restoration plays. Lady Cockwood was ridiculous because she was in a vague sense an interloper, one who pestered the dandies of the *beau monde*. The two country knights were also laughed at, but with less of amused superiority, because they were in a way kindred spirits with the courtly men-about-town. The two girls, Ariana and Gatty, were welcomed with delight, for they possessed the wit which the fashionable circle most prized. Class consciousness, with the inevitable interest in its own manners and amusements, was clearly a formative influence in the play. But this spirit was everywhere tempered by the indifference which belonged to Etheredge's native attitude toward life and which he had been shown how to apply to the comic treatment of mankind by the early success of Molière.

Without going on to consider here Etheredge's further development in *Sir Fopling Flutter* (1676), we may note how different Etheredge is from the Frenchman whose general attitude he followed. I do not refer to the unconcern for moral and social considerations which was mentioned above, nor to the lightness of touch with which he handles comic scenes. In the last respect he is much like Molière. The scenes of *She Would if She Could* in which Ariana and Gatty appear are sprightly and graceful, and the childish conceit and affected fine manners of Sir Fopling in his last play are presented with a gaiety that makes the figure one of the most entertaining in Restoration drama. But with all this ease and liveliness, Etheredge's most animated scenes take a turn that is decidedly unlike Molière's. The Englishman delights in repartee and wit ; he is not so much amused by the incongruities of life as by the sudden juxtaposition of contradictory ideas. Moreover, he looks at life with a strange insensibility. Molière laughed at the ridiculous, but his laughter was not devoid of sympathy. Etheredge, on the contrary, asks us to laugh at the pranks of a roysterer who at midnight arouses with bells and fiddles and boisterous songs the woman he is courting, or at an elegant gallant who, in order to fall into the arms of an heiress, discards the mistress he has at length won with exceeding trouble. It is indeed a heartless world he presents, and he laughs with an entire acquiescence in its point of view. He is thus far from sharing

Molière's attitude that the comic consists in whatever is incongruous with the reasonable demands of society. It should nevertheless be remembered that he approached Molière in lightness of touch and gaiety of spirit, and also that he owed to Molière the conception that manners are interesting on the stage in themselves without being remodeled into humors or obscured by the incidents of a busy plot.

The influence of Molière on Etheredge resulted from the Englishman's witnessing a few of the French pieces on the stage. His influence on Wycherley was due to a close study of the printed works of the Frenchman. It will be recalled that Wycherley spent the most impressionable years of his youth, from fifteen to twenty, in western France in the circle of Madame de Montausier, more famous under her maiden name of Julie de Rambouillet.[1] It was the cult of preciosity with which this circle was associated that Molière attacked in *Les Précieuses Ridicules* in 1659, the last year of Wycherley's stay in France.

[1] Cf. Dennis, *Some Remarkable Passages*, p. 114 f.; Spence, p. 13.

The tremendous sensation which the satire produced on the banks of the Seine must have been reëchoed on the banks of the Charente, so that the young Englishman could hardly forget this new kind of comedy. It is indeed certain that he followed Molière's career eagerly after his return to England and made use of the French comedies in all his own work. This study of the printed plays is evident from the numerous borrowings in his first comedy, *Love in a Wood* (1671).[1] More important, however, is the adoption of Molière's method that appears in the close transcript from contemporary social life. Wycherley's stay in France had enabled him to appreciate how faithfully Molière had copied the widespread affectation of preciosity and how essentially new such method of copying was in French drama. The satiric bent of his own nature took keen pleasure in the ridicule Molière poured out on the fad, but the vehemence of his feelings kept him from ever being able to assume the same attitude

[1] On the date of production of all Wycherley's plays, cf. Klette, p. 30 ff.; Quaas, p. 50 ff.; the notices in the Mermaid edition; and Aitken's article in the *Dictionary of National Biography.*

of detachment toward the affectations he might himself satirize. The consequence was that in scenes from a tavern or St. James's Park or the rooms of a procuress, all done to the life, were placed an alderman made highly ridiculous for the delectation of the aristocratic courtiers and a pretender to wit so silly as to excite unbounded merriment among the worshipers of brilliant conceits. Moreover, the dialogue was filled with witty observations in which the author expressed his individual scorn of some features of the London life he was copying. This was not only unlike Etheredge's careless indifference, but entirely foreign to Molière's philosophic aloofness.

It would be interesting to determine whether Wycherley began his imitation of Molière independently or as a result of Etheredge's innovation. According to Wycherley's own account, he composed *Love in a Wood* even before the Restoration. It is impossible to accept the declaration, not only because the borrowings from Molière are from plays produced after the Restoration, but because the society reflected in the comedy is already

pretty well developed.   In the prologue the
author declares he

> is come to suffer here to-day
> For counterfeiting (as you judge) a play.[1]

This has generally been considered a reference
to Sedley's *Mulberry Garden*, a tragi-comedy
produced in 1668.   The comic plot is of the
intrigue variety, but the influence of *Love in a
Tub*, and possibly of *She Would if She Could*,
appears in several passages where the life
of the time is pretty fully transcribed.   Still,
Wycherley's play is in no sense a counterfeit
of Sedley's or of either of Etheredge's, and he
certainly could not be referring to the French
plays from which he borrowed.   Sedley had
centered the interest in the windings of the
plot, but Wycherley interested his audience
in figures that were easily recognized as typical
in spite of their farcical coloring and in scenes
that were obviously copied from the London
of the day.   He was thus doing the same
thing as Etheredge.   All the antecedent prob-
abilities therefore favor the supposition that
he was stimulated to imitate Molière by

[1] Wycherley, p. 9.

Etheredge's example, but the original manner of his imitation renders it impossible to declare with certainty that he was not independent of that example.

Possibly the most familiar incident [1] in Wycherley's life arose from the success of his first play. The Duchess of Cleveland, who as Lady Castlemain and the King's mistress had excited the interest of Pepys, leaned halfway out of her coach one day to accost the dramatist as he was passing. He was enough of a gallant to walk immediately into her favor and into the high esteem of her circle, so much so that the King himself manifested a remarkable interest in Wycherley's welfare. There may be a trace of royal influence in his basing his second play, *The Gentleman Dancing Master* (1671), on a Spanish original. The comedy shows that the beaux and wits had developed the spirit of a clique, definite and self-conscious, and at the same time were liberating themselves from foreign influence, so that the witless Paris was laughed at for his adoption of extravagant French costume

[1] Cf. Dennis, *Some Remarkable Passages*, p. 115 ff.; Spence, p. 13.

as much as the austerely grave Don Diego for his assumption of Spanish manners.   The ideals of the set were even more clearly defined in *The Country Wife* (1673), where the effort of an old rake to keep a country girl all to himself after marriage was found highly ridiculous, the reiterated pretensions of fine ladies to strict virtue were discovered to be nothing but a cloak for the more secure enjoyment of forbidden fruit, and the fatuous conceit of a would-be wit was humiliated to bless the true wit of the play with the only good woman among the *dramatis personæ.*

Without considering *The Plain Dealer*, which was produced the next year, we can see clearly that the explanation of Wycherley's popularity is to be found in the faithfulness with which he reflected the attitude of the worldly society which controlled the taste of the play-going public.   He had learned well the lesson of *Les Précieuses Ridicules.* He had learned how to employ his keen native sense of the comic so as to appeal most directly to the spirit of the clique which already characterized the Restoration.   How genuine his feeling for comedy was may be

seen in *The Gentleman Dancing Master*, where
the determination of Don Diego never to
admit that he has been fooled and the in-
sistence of Mrs. Caution on her superior pene-
tration furnish as laughable scenes as the
period has to show. But it is likewise to be
noted that Wycherley added a special appeal
to his audience by giving to the man a
ridiculous affectation of Spanish gravity and
to the woman a suspicion of Puritan prin-
ciples. He had learned his lesson well, as I
have said, but no one who knows anything
of psychology will expect that he reproduced
Molière's method and attitude unaltered.
He was an Englishman, and a very independent Englishman at that. The fine sense
of proportion which is at the bottom of
Molière's comedy could never be assimilated
by a man of such a vigorous nature as Wycherley's. The violence of *The Plain Dealer*
was merely a development from the exaggeration to which he resorted in *Love in a Wood*
to render his farcical figures ridiculous. He
had, moreover, a love of satire essentially
different from the sympathy which tinges
Molière's aloofness. He delighted to fill

whole pages with keen and flashing wit directed at the various customs and hypocrisies of the day. But in this, too, he was reflecting his time. He was in reality as much a man of his age as Molière was of the age of Louis XIV.

These few plays produced between 1664 and 1674 brought into the Restoration theater the new comedy of manners. *Love in a Tub* was frequently revived.[1] At the first performance of *Sho Would if She Could* a thousand people were turned away, though its promise of popularity was largely defeated by poor acting.[2] *Love in a Wood* was a great success.[3] *The Gentleman Dancing Master* did not take,[4] but it was followed by *The Country Wife*, one of the most influential comedies of the whole period, and by *The Plain Dealer*, which elicited high praise from the Laureate himself.[5] The nature of the impression made by these plays coming out in rapid succession

[1] Cf. Downes, p. 32 ; Etheredge, p. x, note 2.

[2] Cf. Pepys, vii. 287 (Feb. 6, 1667–8); Shadwell, *Works*, i. 118 f.

[3] Cf. dedication, and Dennis, *Some Remarkable Passages*, p. 115.

[4] Cf. Downes, p. 32.

[5] Cf. Dryden, *Works*, v. 115.

is plainly seen in contemporary comedy. Shadwell's *Sullen Lovers* (1668) had been a close imitation of Jonson's comedy of humors, but *The Miser* (1671) reflected the new development with unmistakable clearness. Crowne's *Country Wit* (1675) carried on the type. The playwrights had learned to attain success by appealing to the sense of recognition, either in its purity, or with only the slightest tinge of satire, or with the admixture of satire made acrid with the strongest gall.

Even more noteworthy was the influence on Dryden. He was not dowered with a true sense of comedy, more than once expressing his contempt for it,[1] but he had an unerring sense for changes in public taste. During the first ten years, when Fletcher and Jonson were constantly revived and when the King's fondness for Spanish drama was well known, he produced humors and comedies of intrigue. The success of Etheredge and Wycherley opened his eyes to a new side of the Molière from whom he had been borrowing. His lack of familiarity with French conditions had prevented him from noting the essential

[1] Cf. *e.g.*, Dryden, *Works*, iii. 240.

realism of Molière's satiric pictures. Naturally, *Sir Martin Mar-All* (1667), founded on *L'Étourdi*, was a comedy of intrigue. But it was not so natural to introduce into *An Evening's Love* (1668), also a comedy of intrigue, the rôle of Aurelia, a Jonsonian humor suggested by Molière's several paintings of preciosity. *Marriage à la Mode* (1672) is a different kind of piece with different figures. Recognizing the validity of the ridicule of heroic plays in *The Rehearsal* (1671), Dryden apparently considered it advisable to compress a plot originally intended to fill five acts with heroic incident and rant. The half thus left vacant he filled with a satiric picture of Restoration life, in which the influence of Molière, *She Would if She Could* and *Love in a Wood*, is unmistakable. For the first time in Dryden the interest is centered in the social criticism, even though the scenes contain as many signs of literary reminiscence as of personal observation. Besides, Melantha is not a humor of the kind he had been presenting, interesting chiefly as an oddity, a curiosity. She is the reproduction, in much Molière's spirit, of female foppery and an extravagance in the employment of French phrases which was common at the time, and she is interesting precisely because she is such a copy or re-production. Of course, Dryden's dramatic method had been formed in the ten years preceding the date of this piece, and he never gained a genuine interest in the realistic satire of society. By assiduous flattery he had entered the circle of wits and beaux, but his inspiration came, not from their society, but from literary sources. He therefore did not fully understand the secret of Molière's success, but in all his later use of bor-rowed material he did keep the French master before his eyes.

Thus at the end of the first decade of the Restoration the comedy of manners developed in France by Molière was transplanted to England, where it grew as best it could in the thin soil and murky atmosphere of King Charles's court.

CHAPTER IV

THE ATTITUDE TOWARD MOLIÈRE

THE influence of Molière, unmistakably present in *Love in a Tub* in 1664, really effected a change in Restoration drama with the series of plays beginning in 1668, when the society necessary for any comedy of manners had developed class-consciousness and unity of feeling. But Etheredge was not the first man to adapt material from Molière. It was Davenant who made the first borrowing, in *The Playhouse to be Let* (1663),[1] which is in reality a series of extended dramatic sketches. In the first act the audience learns that some players must let their theater for the vacation and that four companies are to present sketches in competition for the privilege of renting the house. These four separate pieces fill the remaining four acts of the play. The second company to appear, which is supposed to

[1] On the date of production, cf. Davenant, iv. 3.

have lately come over from France, very naturally presents *Sganarelle ou le Cocu Imaginaire*, translated into broken English to render the supposition more convincing. Davenant follows the original closely, retaining a good deal of the animation. The only changes in the action, due to the omission of three scenes and parts of the long speeches, are that the servant of the young lover does not appear, that the man who imagines his wife has become unfaithful does not consult her relatives, and that the wife and young lover remain on the porch instead of entering the house. The original being comedy of intrigue, this translation does not belong to Restoration comedy of manners, but it is interesting to note how early Molière was laid under contribution to provide gaiety for London audiences.

It is significant that the first borrowing was this piece rather than *Les Précieuses Ridicules*. In this selection Davenant was representative of the minor playwrights of the whole period, who regarded Molière merely as a public storehouse of plots, incidents, and characters. Caryll pretty certainly had in mind the recent borrowing from Molière as

well as from other sources when he wrote a
caustic passage in the epilogue to his own
adaptation of *L'École des Femmes* (1669–70):—

> Faith, be good natur'd to this hungry Crew,
> Who, what they filch abroad, bring home to you.
>
> But still exclude those Men from all Relief,
> Who steal themselves, yet boldly cry, Stop Thief ;
> Like taking Judges, these without Remorse
> Condemn all petty Thefts, and practice worse ;
> As if they Robb'd by Patent, and alone
> Had right to call each Foreign Play their own.
>
> What we have brought before you, was not meant
> For a new Play, but a new President ;
> For we with Modesty our Theft avow,
> (There is some Conscience us'd in stealing too)
> And openly declare, that if our Choer
> Does hit your Pallats, you must thank Molliere.[1]

A decade later Molière's dramas had been so
frequently resorted to that Thomas Durfey
asked in a song appearing in *Sir Barnaby
Whig* (1681),

> Molière is quite rifled, then how shall I write? [2]

An equally suggestive piece of evidence occurs
at the very end of the period. Corey's *Metamorphosis* was published in 1704 as "Written
Originally by the Famous Moliere," when in

---

[1] Cf. epilogue to *Sir Salomon.*
[2] Cf. Kerby, p. iii.

reality it owed absolutely nothing to him. It was merely a reworking, with very close paraphrase in many places, of Tomkis's *Albumazar*, an academic play popular in Jacobean times.[1]   Other evidence that Molière was still plundered is afforded by Brown's *Stage-Beaux tossed in a Blanket*, published in the same year and intended as a reply to Collier's *Short View of the Immorality and Profaneness of the English Stage.* Though Brown had been writing satire most of his life, he apparently felt unequal to inventing a plot sufficiently biting or sarcastic for an attack on Collier, since in the first and third acts of this farce he adapted part of *La Critique de l'École des Femmes* and a scene from *Le Tartuffe.* Brown recognized the satiric element in Molière much more distinctly than most of the minor dramatists of the age, but his play was entirely typical in one respect : it indicates how persistent was the

[1] It is easy to explain the few similarities that exist between *Metamorphosis* and *L'Avare.* *Albumazar* was based on Porta's *L'Astrologo* (cf. Smith, p. 566, and the reference there given), which in turn must owe a good deal to *Aulularia.* The play of Plautus was the source of several features of *L'Avare.* The similarities are thus due to a common ultimate source.

belief that Molière afforded the most convenient source for almost any kind of material the dramatist might need.

The attitude of these men being that of
the practical playwright, who makes no effort
to reproduce tho spirit of the original, but
spends all his time in adapting the material
to his audience, their borrowing naturally
assumed a variety of forms. Often whole
scenes were lifted from their French context
and inserted in some English play with only
the necessary changes. It was in this
fashion that Congreve among the leaders
made use of a famous scene in *Don Juan*
for the opening of *Love for Love*. Among
ephemeral plays, the opening of Sedley's
Mulberry Garden was similarly taken from
L'École des Maris. Singularly enough, no
further assistance was derived from the
French piece except in so far as the two
brothers thus introduced continued throughout the action. Such use of adapted or suggested characters was a second form which
borrowing assumed. The subject, too large
for discussion here, will be treated at length
in a later chapter, but it may not be out of

place to note that in this matter, as in others,
the minor dramatists were not studying the
French genius as a master, but were delving
into his works just as Scarron and Rotrou
delved into the inexhaustible mine of Spanish comedy. They consequently took from
Molière whatever incidents, situations, types,
and characters struck their fancy. For they
would have found incomprehensible the present estimate of Molière as one of the greatest
comic geniuses, so that they were never influenced by the respect for their source as
a work of art which would guide an English
adaptor in handling *Die Versunkene Glocke*
or *El Gran Galeoto*. It is therefore only fair
to judge them by their success in making
the borrowed material suit their purposes.
For they were obliged to observe the principle enunciated in my first chapter, that the
comic sense is by no means a fixed quantity,
and while a Restoration wit did not differ
in taste from a wealthy bourgeois under
Louis XIV as much as a Hottentot would
from a New Yorker, the difference was great
enough to render imperative a considerable
alteration in nearly any French play that

was to succeed at Drury Lane or Lincoln's
Inn Fields. They had the further justifi-
cation, that they generally selected parts of
Molière's lighter plays and comedies of intrigue in preference to his masterpieces.

Among the larger forms of borrowing translation as close as Davenant's was extremely
rare. Indeed, the only similar productions
were Dryden's *Amphitryon*, Otway's *Cheats
of Scapin*, Vanbrugh's *Mistake*, and Medbourne's *Tartuffe*. Medbourne was willing
to be credited with great admiration for *Le
Tartuffe*, but he would very likely have been
puzzled to explain the grounds of his estimate in the dedication : —

My Lord, I Here Present your Honour with the
Master-Piece of Molière's Productions, or rather of all
French Comedy. What considerable Additionals I
have made thereto, in order to its more plausible Appearance on the English Theatre, I leave to be observ'd
by those who shall give themselves the trouble of comparing the several Editions of this Comedy.

The plausibility he refers to concerns the *dénouement*. In Molière the outcome is in
suspense until the end, when the power of
the King intervenes to avert the ruin hanging

over Orgon. Medbourne develops an intrigue between Laurence (corresponding to Tartuffe's servant, Laurent, who does not appear on the stage in the original), and the maid Dorina, whereby the estate conveyed to Tartuffe is returned to the giver and the other persons are warned in time to secure the assistance of King and council in worsting the hypocrite. This intrigue is of course closed by the marriage of the participants. Medbourne gives full measure in marriages by having the lover Valere promise his sister, unheard of in the French, to the boyish and impetuous Damis. These changes, however, are insignificant compared with the addition at the close, where the characters join in a dance ! A partial explanation of why Medbourne missed the spirit of the original so far is suggested by a specimen or two of his translation. Not only is the idiom "avoir raison" rendered by "have right," but expressions such as "ces galants de cour dont les femmes sont folles" [1] appear in English as "Courtly Gallants whose foolish prating

---

[1] Which may be rendered colloquially: "Those court gallants the women are so crazy about."

wives." A more wretched misconception of
meaning results in giving "ravel me back to
my first nothing" for "vos bontés . . .
jusqu'à mon néant daignent se ravaler." [1]
All this striving for faithfulness is embodied
in the worst blank verse ever spoken in an
English theater. When Molière's most powerful and poetic speeches are rendered in this
style, it is a matter of no significance that the
translator betrays respect for the "Master-
Piece . . . of all French Comedy" by omitting
only some half-dozen scenes. Dryden's *Amphitryon* is of course much more worthy of
the original, but not so representative of the
period. Medbourne's peculiarity is not that
he lowered the tone of Molière's comedy, but
that he made any effort to retain the integrity and spirit of the original.

Translation, however, was far less frequent
than adaptation. The commonest form was
the combining of two or more plots in order
to satisfy the English demand for action, but
there were various methods of effecting this
combination. Ravenscroft would sit down

[1] Freely translated: "Your kindness condescends to
my worthless state."

with a long pair of shears, a large pot of paste, and two or three of Molière's comedies, and after much cutting out and ingenious pasting together would produce a most bewildering scrap-book farce. Dryden would read over carefully several plays, one of them preferably Spanish, revolve the various incidents in his capacious memory, and after long musing evolve a new course of action in which the best situations would reappear with a modified set of *dramatis personæ*. A more minute examination of a representative play will indicate the spirit in which the adaptations were made.

The Dumb Lady (1669) of John Lacy, the actor, will serve the purpose as well as any. The play consists of more episodes than can well be taken into account, but the main plot may be summarized thus : Drench, a farrier, beats his wife in a quarrel, and she in revenge persuades two men who are hunting for a physician that he is the greatest in the world, though it takes a beating to make him admit it. They accordingly beat him into an admission and take him to old Gernette, whose daughter Olinda has recently been struck dumb at a very inopportune time, since it prevents her marriage with Squire Softhead, a foolish countryman whom her father has selected because the squire's estate surrounds his. After at length prescribing treatment for Olinda, Drench meets Leander, Olinda's lover, whom he is prevailed upon to introduce into Gernette's house as his apothecary.

Up to this point Lacy followed *Le Médecin malgré lui* closely, but it was obviously inadvisable to follow it further, since to do so would close his play with the third act. A very simple method of expanding it to five acts presented itself — to adapt *L'Amour Médecin* for the remainder of the play. This he accomplished in the following manner: —

Drench effects a cure of Olinda's dumbness, which of course has been all pretense, but he has her feign madness in order that there may be some ground for asking her removal to his apothecary's house. The suspicious father will hear nothing of the plan, and even ejects the two rogues from the house as impostors. They secure reinstatement by handing over an alleged letter of Leander, and at once join in a consultation of physicians that Gernette has called to consider his daughter's case. Then it is necessary that Drench play the part of the doctor, instead of the lover's playing it, as in *L'Amour Médecin*. The consultation is also altered by the fact that Drench must sustain his pretensions before actual physicians. This is one reason for the introduction of Othentic, a brother of Leander who is in orders and who is of great assistance to Drench in hoodwinking the doctors. Having come out victorious over the genuine physicians, Drench declares that the only way to cure Olinda's insanity is to humor her prepossessions by pretending to marry her to his apothecary. Here we find a further reason for introducing Othentic, that he may take the part of the *notaire* in the original and unite the two in marriage.

Clearly, then, *Le Médecin malgré lui* is the basis of the play and furnishes the incidents of the first three acts, in the first two of which the original is followed closely. *L'Amour Médecin* furnishes the incidents for the last two acts, but the alterations are considerable owing to the adjustment with the plot of the preceding divisions.

Even the combining of the two plots did not give as much briskness to his play as Lacy thought necessary. He accordingly presented a number of minor actions or episodes. The first and most important of these was already partly developed in *Le Médecin malgré lui* in the scenes between the mock-doctor Sganarelle and the nurse Jacqueline. Those scenes were far too tame for Lacy; he not only made the dialogue licentious, but he easily converted the action into an intrigue of the lowest kind, the nurse with very little reluctance proving false to her husband. The husband, Jarvis, in a measure gets even with her by entering into similar relations with Drench's wife, who has followed the quack, but whom that now famous doctor has refused to own, even having her locked up in a cage to get rid of her importunities. She and Jarvis together attempt to expose Drench, but he retaliates by securing her confinement in a madhouse. The humor of the scene is undeniable, but it owes nothing to Molière. Another source of comic effect employed from time to time is the illicit relations existing between the nurse and

Gernette. One might suppose the intrigue now confused enough to suit even the most fastidious Restoration audience, but such a supposition would prove the reader unacquainted with this kind of play. Another episode that fills several scenes is developed from *Le Médecin malgré lui*. The rival of Léandre does not appear in Molière, but Lacy exhibits him at full length in Softhead, a conventional figure in the plays of the period. There has been an attempt at a duel between Leander and Softhead, in which the latter has distinguished himself by his arrant cowardice. He accidentally meets Leander after that redoubtable antagonist and resourceful young lover has assumed the disguise of an apothecary. When Leander sees he is not recognized, he frightens the cully into paying two hundred pounds by reporting that Leander is nearing death from the wounds received. The humor is increased by the fact that Softhead not only has to pay, but has afterward to confess that he ran away from the encounter.

The episode indicates how quick an eye Lacy had for a situation and thus explains his recognition of Molière as a rich source of comic incidents. For Molière as the penetrating student of manners and character he found no use, and even for Molière as a master of farce he held none too exalted an opinion. He made no effort to reproduce the comic spirit of the plays he was adapting. Drench, for example, was made a farrier instead of a wood-cutter in order to render the action more plausible. Molière was attacking the medical profession and of a purpose made the mock-doctor Sganarelle the most good-for-nothing person imaginable. Lacy, having no such satiric aim, retained only so much of the ridicule as would seem funny on general grounds, and rendered the action more likely by raising the doctor in the social scale. There is, moreover, a persistent effort to lower the tone of the original to the level which Lacy's experience as an actor had taught him would best suit a Restoration audience. In the first place, most of the important changes in character should be ascribed to the adaptor's search for indecency. The quarrel between Drench and his wife near the beginning arises over her unfaithfulness;

she proudly declares that but one of her four children is the farrier's. Even the supposedly pure characters are made to furnish the same kind of amusement. Olinda, while not impure, is not exactly a model of delicacy; she is disappointed when Leander says they are to have only eight children, and in her pretended madness she addresses her father with a coarseness totally unthinkable in the Lucinde of the original. In the second place, Lacy inserts a great many dialogues which have no value for characterization and do not advance the action, but which are so thoroughly seasoned with the spice of ribaldry that they must have tickled the palates of the Restoration theater-goers in exactly the way to give them zest for the whole play.

Very clearly, then, Lacy had definitely decided that there were two sure roads to popularity. They were, not to reproduce the atmosphere and spirit of Molière's comedy, but to introduce as much intrigue as possible, in order to hold the attention by briskness of movement, and to infuse into the play a great deal of wanton incident and licentious dialogue. He produced not only a complete adaptation, but a typical illustration of the attitude toward Molière prevailing among the second-rate dramatists.

Among men of greater distinction there was a third class of borrowings, which consisted in little more than the use of suggestions. The plot of *The English Friar*, for example, is developed from the main points in *Le Tartuffe*, but to call Crowne's play an adaptation is to use the term in a loose sense. Sometimes only a single scene is thus developed. In *Love Triumphant* a nurse brings in two children just when the light o' love Dalinda is about to secure a husband. In *Monsieur de Pourceaugnac* the title character, who has come all the way from Limoges to Paris to marry the daughter of Oronte, is confronted in Oronte's presence by two women who pretend to have married him in the provinces and who bring in children to support their assertions. The common elements are obvious enough, but the surrounding circumstances are so different that, if borrowings from Molière were not numerous in Dryden, one would hesitate to affirm that the French situation is the suggestion for the English scene.

The inference to be drawn from these various translations, adaptations, and instances of suggestion is clear : the second-rate dramatist of the period did not consider the Frenchman as any more a master of play-writing than himself, and found him in constant need of improvement for English audiences. But we are not dependent on inference alone in estimating the rank accorded to Molière during the Restoration. Direct statements abound. A few dramatists, like Medbourne,[1] place Molière very high. Caryll in 1670 speaks of him as

> the Famous Shakspear of this Age,
> Both when he Writes, and when he treads the Stage.[2]

Wright in 1693 refers to him as "the great Original of French Comedy."[3] Both of these estimates, however, come from men of taste who had a literary, not a practical, interest in Molière. They wrote plays once in a while for diversion, not as fast as they could for bread and butter. The minor playwrights, who knew Restoration audiences and who

[1] Cf. dedication to *Tartuffe*.
[2] Cf. epilogue to *Sir Salomon*.
[3] Cf. dedication to *The Female Virtuosoes*.

were eager to please them, assumed a very complacent, patronizing air toward the author of *Le Misanthrope*. Shadwell in the preface to his *Miser* (1671) has this to say of his indebtedness : —

The Foundation of this Play I took from one of Moliere's, call'd *L'Avare;* but that having too few Persons, and too little Action for an English Theatre, I added to both so much, that I may call more than half of this Play my own; and I think I may say without Vanity, that Moliere's Part of it has not suffer'd in my Hands ; nor did I ever know a French Comedy made use of by the worst of our Poets, that was not better'd by 'em. 'Tis not Barrenness of Wit or Invention, that makes us borrow from the French, but Laziness; and this was the Occasion of my making Use of *L'Avare*.[1]

At the close of the period Mrs. Centlivre sums up the feeling with equal definiteness : —

Some Scenes I confess are partly taken from Moliere, and I dare be bold to say it has not suffered in the Translation : I thought 'em pretty in the French, and cou'd not help believing they might divert in an English Dress. The French have that light Airiness in their Temper, that the least Glimpse of Wit sets them a laughing, when 'twou'd not make us so much as smile ; so that when I found the stile too poor, I endeavoured to give it a Turn ; for whoever borrows from them, must take care to

[1] Shadwell, *Works*, iii. 7.

touch the Colours with an English Pencil, and form the Piece according to our Manners.[1]

Even the leading dramatists, the men who were most profoundly influenced by the genius across the Channel, were not at all disposed to acknowledge their indebtedness. Congreve nowhere avowed his study of Molière, and Dryden carefully refrained from giving intimation of how thoroughly he had read the Frenchman's comedies. In the *Essay of Dramatic Poesy* Molière is mentioned, but only for his alleged imitation of the English or his boldness in using prose.[2]

The conclusion is obvious. The minor playwrights of the Restoration, who borrowed from Molière oftener and in more wholesale fashion than any other author, except perhaps Lope de Vega, has ever been borrowed from, seldom recognized the greatness of the Frenchman's genius. In general they regarded him, not as a master of the comic to be studied for his view of life or his dramaturgic skill, but as a storehouse of plots, scenes, and characters to be adapted to the

[1] Cf. preface to *Love's Contrivance.*
[2] Cf. Dryden, *Works*, xv. 330, 354.

well-known taste of the Restoration audiences. The modern estimate of Molière as not only the greatest comic dramatist of France but as one of the few comic geniuses of the world, would have seemed to them the veriest nonsense. He was merely a popular comedian whose plays were mighty good sources for material, provided always the material was improved for the more exacting English taste. This attitude explains the influence of Molière on the mass of ephemeral comedy of the age. The leading dramatists caught something of the spirit of Molière's comedy of manners, but the minor playwrights saw in him only the clever manipulator of a comedy of intrigue.

CHAPTER V

It will be remembered that of the three classes into which I divided Molière's plays, the comedy of intrigue was merely a continuation of the type up to that time dominant in France. Indeed, the type was ancient and widespread. Passing over the New Comedy of Greece, of which too little is known even since the most recent discoveries, one will recall that the work of Plautus and Terence was largely of this variety. A common plot was the schemes of a resourceful and unscrupulous slave to secure to the young hero a mistress from the hands of some rapacious and hard-hearted procurer. This intriguing servant was inherited by the Italian comedy of masks, and often the plots of Latin plays, as well as stories from *novelle*, and at a later period imbroglios from the Spanish *comedia*, were adapted for the scenarios tacked up in the theater behind the scenes for the guidance of the improvising actors.[1] But the intrigue of Plautus was hardly sufficient for a public which had little interest in anything but movement, so that suggestions for minor intrigues were frequently developed in somewhat the same way that Lacy developed such suggestion in *Le Médecin malgré lui*.[2] The action thereby became a loose and confusing combination of stratagems. While the *commedia dell' arte* was reaching the height of its popularity in Italy and France, Lope de Vega and his followers were developing the famous comedy of cloak and sword in Spain. In it, too, the playwright's effort was to construct a maze of incident which should keep the audience perpetually guessing what was to come next, but the unrivaled ingeniousness of the Spaniard produced plots which were at once intricate and compact. The story unrolled itself with many turns and counterturns, so that the playgoer was kept wondering till the very close exactly how the author

[1] Cf. Bartoli, introduzione.

[2] Cf. *ante*, p. 88 ff. For the way in which the *Pseudolus* of Plautus was thus adapted, cf. Scherillo, p. 121 ff.

was going to bring the loving pairs into each other's arms. Equally skilful was the interweaving of different lines of action. The spectator seldom became conscious of the separateness of the parts, for episodic figures, such as Don Mendo and Nuño in *El Alcalde de Zalamea*,[1] were extremely rare in the Spanish *comedia*. It will be recalled that the *comedia* was transplanted to France during the youth of Molière, but the form which influenced him most was the *commedia dell' arte*, with which he became familiar in his provincial journeyings. His first play, *L'Étourdi*, may be taken as a brilliant development of that type.

The minor dramatists of the Restoration had exactly the same end in view as the Italians and Spaniards — to hold the attention of the audience by abundant movement. This effort was no new thing in England. Kyd in his *Spanish Tragedy* made large use of the same kind of appeal, and Fletcher employed it constantly. The Restoration playwrights were gifted neither with the inventiveness requisite for devising incidents in a compli-

[1] Of course this play does not belong to the cloak-and-sword type.

cated stratagem nor with power to construct
a coherent plot out of material already at
hand. Some of them frankly recognized their
weakness by translating foreign plays. Tuke's
Adventures of Five Hours was taken from
Calderon with apparently no changes in plot.
Otway, who in comedy must be placed with
the ephemeral writers, likewise translated *Les
Fourberies de Scapin* with very few alterations. Other men, however, found even the
most vivacious pieces of Molière too slow for
the more exacting taste of Englishmen, and
accordingly "improved" his efforts. Of this
class was Edward Ravenscroft, so inveterate
a plagiarist that when he no longer found anything good in Molière or other Frenchmen,
he plagiarized from his own earlier plagiarisms.

His first play, *Mamamouchi* (1671), is typical of his method. The main action is made
up of several parts. Mr. Jorden, a citizen
whose wealth has turned his head to the extent that he now sets up for a gentleman
and takes lessons in music, dancing, and
fencing, is determined that his daughter Lucia
shall marry into the aristocracy, and accordingly has chosen a foolish country knight,

Sir Simon Softhead, for his son-in-law.
Lucia's lover, Cleverwit, plans and executes
a number of projects to win her : (1) with the
help of some "men of intrigue" he succeeds
in disgusting Sir Simon with London and Lucia;
(2) at the same time he disgusts Mr. Jorden
with the knight ; (3) he then wins Lucia
by disguising himself as the Grand Turk, in
which character he is acceptable to Mr.
Jorden. This action is drawn from several
sources. The depiction of Mr. Jorden's folly
is taken from the first three acts of *Le Bourgeois Gentilhomme*. The first two of Cleverwit's intrigues are a reproduction of *Monsieur
de Pourceaugnac*. The third is a copy of the
Turkish masquerade scenes in *Le Bourgeois
Gentilhomme*. This procedure surely betrays
no effort to reproduce Molière's dramatic
structure.

There is a second action almost as important
as the first. Mr. Jorden's son is in love with
Marina, a girl whom his father intends to
marry. He accordingly schemes to win her
from his father by having a sempstress masquerade as a German princess, whom Mr.
Jorden of course prefers on account of her

rank. He also wishes to secure money from
his father. Cureall, a man of intrigue, does
this for a time by pretending to be a doctor
intimate at court. Later the son gets his
father's whole estate by making use of Cleverwit's disguise as the Grand Turk ; the father
is so much pleased at being made a *mamamouchi* that by the advice of another rogue
he settles his entire fortune on his son in order
to live with the Sultan. This action, too, has
several sources. The device of making the
father and son rivals is taken from *L'Avare.*
Cureall's disguise is an adaptation of the rôle
of Dorante in *Le Bourgeois Gentilhomme,* and
the Turkish scenes are of course from the same
play. Betty Trickmore's disguise as a German princess is a reminiscence of Frosine's
plan in *L'Avare* or of *Les Précieuses Ridicules.*

The plot as a whole, then, is a combination of *Le Bourgeois Gentilhomme* and *Monsieur de Pourceaugnac,* with an important
addition from *L'Avare* and a hint from *Les
Précieuses Ridicules.* The two actions are
bound together by the rogues, Cureall and
Trickmore, who appear in both, and also by
having Sir Simon, the country knight of the

first part, marry Betty Trickmore, the reputed German princess of the second part. The Englishman displayed considerable ingenuity in thus piecing together the shreds and patches taken from the work of the great Frenchman.

But the full ingeniousness of Ravenscroft's method doth not yet appear. He did not borrow only the incidents from his sources. He borrowed most of the dialogue, too. When he did not translate he paraphrased, making only such changes as his complicated plot and the English scene demanded. He simply altered the dialect of a Flemish merchant to that of a man from Norwich, and instead of a count who was an accomplished scoundrel he introduced a rogue who used the same speeches in the disguise of a court physician. By such means he saved himself the trouble of writing nine-tenths of the dialogue, and in the remaining tenth he followed more or less closely some scene in Molière as a model.

The whole extent of the "improvement" becomes clear on considering the *dramatis personæ* in this salmagundi of situations. Ravenscroft's Mr. Jorden is of course M.

Jourdain through most of the play, but in many scenes he has to act the part of Oronte in *Monsieur de Pourceaugnac*. Clearly, this concocter of a pure comedy of intrigue felt no disagreement between Molière's masterly delineation of the folly of middle-class ambition and his sketch of a typical self-centered father. He even thought it proper to have M. Jourdain play the part of Harpagon by preparing to marry a young woman with no pretensions to aristocracy! He thus with a very small expenditure of energy was able to produce a very busy course of action. If commercial success be a criterion, he was perfectly justified.[1]

Further illustrations are unnecessary to show that the hack writers of the period were not following Molière or the Spanish in plot-structure. The Englishmen, to be sure, were resorting to the same means of holding an audience. That is one reason why they adapted so frequently the disguise employed in *Les Précieuses Ridicules*[2] and why they

[1] Cf. Downes, p. 32.

[2] Besides the play by Ravenscroft considered above, cf. Behn's *False Count*, Shadwell's *Bury Fair*, Betterton's *Amorous Widow*, Congreve's *Way of the World*.

borrowed from time to time a good many
devices and situations from the Spanish.
But they were far from displaying the skill
of Molière or Lope de Vega in interlacing the
different actions.   Such skill would have been
impossible to them in any event, but as a
matter of fact they did not strive for that kind
of structure.   They sought not only to produce much action, but to introduce many persons.   Their method was more like that of
Fletcher and the Jacobeans, whose plays were
constantly revived during the early Restoration.   Fletcher was indeed a man of great
ingenuity, but the intrigues in his plays were
often quite distinct and always easily sepa-
rable, and the scene was thronged with actors.
The Restoration writers, no matter what the
source of their incidents, put plots together
in the same way, only with less cleverness.
Mrs. Behn in *Sir Patient Fancy* produced just
as confusing a set of stratagems and *dramatis
personæ* in her use of *Le Malade Imaginaire*
as Thomas Durfey did in *Madam Fickle* in
taking suggestions from Marston, Mayne,
and other pre-Restoration playwrights.   But
the illustrations I have given from Lacy and

Ravenscroft are sufficient to indicate the characteristics of a typical Restoration plot.

Among the leading dramatists, also, this type of plot prevailed. They, too, sought to fill the scene with as much movement as possible and to provide an interesting variety of persons. Wycherley adapted *Le Misanthrope* by adding several new lines of action. Dryden in *Limberham*, while professing to write social satire in imitation of *Le Tartuffe*, spun as tangled a skein of incidents as the period has to offer. Congreve in his first play spent a deal of time in making his plot complex, and he succeeded in making it so confusing that no one can remember it. The truth is, the Restoration audiences, though interested in manners, were interested only in the superficial aspect of manners, and consequently had to be entertained with the constant coming and going of actors and the frequent alternation of suspense and surprise.

In a previous chapter I made a distinction between Molière's comedy of intrigue and the comedy which is distinctively his — the comedy of manners and character. In this class he employed a different kind of structure.

He did not endeavor to give many turns and counter-turns to the story, to arouse suspense anew when the play seemed about to end, to render everything again doubtful when all mistakes and misunderstandings were apparently to be cleared up, to bring the intrigue to a sudden close when the confusion was at its height. He now invented or adapted an action which should reveal the character or develop the social question he wished to present. The plot evolved itself from the interplay of character, and moved forward in a single line, with clear motivation, to a logical outcome. The interest was centered, not in movement and bustle, but in the controlling idea and the dominating character. It was consonant with this interest that the conditions in which Molière set his action were adjusted with the greatest nicety to the theme with which each play dealt. The circle of learned ladies where Philaminte defies all her husband's notions concerning the sphere of woman, the bourgeois home where Tartuffe commands as director of conscience, the salon of the accomplished woman of the world where Alceste fumes at the insincerities of life — all these settings show how fine and profound an artist Molière was.

What I have said about the Restoration comedy of intrigue makes it unnecessary to remark that such simplicity of structure was not to be found in England, even among the leading dramatists of the period. Dryden, I have already observed, formed his dramatic method under Spanish influences. His characters in many cases were, under the influence of Molière, made typical of some ridiculous pretension of the times, but his plots were never constructed so that the action should present a retributive judgment that would by itself express the author's criticism of society. It was this method of enforcing a thesis, handled with the impartiality of a true artist, that the author of *Le Misanthrope* constantly employed in his comedy of character. In *L'École des Maris*, Ariste, the indulgent guardian, is made happy in the end with the hand of his ward, while his brother, the severe Sganarelle, is humiliatingly repaid for his severity by losing his ward to the young rival he has treated through most of the play with self-satisfied commiseration. Likewise

Arnolphe of *L'École des Femmes*, who has gone to absurd extremes to insure fidelity in his wife-to-be, wins nothing but anxiety from all his precautions, and is at the close forced to give this intended wife to a young wooer. Dryden paid no attention to this feature of the Frenchman's art, but Wycherley, where he was copying Molière, did introduce a kind of poetic justice to teach some social lesson. In *The Country Wife*, for example, Pinchwife, a worn-out rake, who, in imitation of Arnolphe, is made to marry a country girl in order to be sure he will have one woman all to himself, is in the end doomed to share her with Horner. Wycherley did this not merely because events in the original were arranged similarly, but because he wished to enforce a view of woman, for he presented a contrasting action to emphasize the point. But he did not use the method consistently. Lady Fidget, against whom he repeatedly directed his satire, is in the last scene placed where she can carry on her practices indefinitely. In *The Plain Dealer*, again, Freeman, though put down in the *dramatis personæ* as a complier with the age and delineated as the antithesis of Wycherley's ideal presented in Manly, is allowed to accomplish his plans exactly as he wishes. In short, it is clear that Wycherley did not entirely adopt, along with Molière's satiric attitude toward contemporary manners, the Frenchman's method of constructing a plot.

A similar statement may be made of Congreve. Lady Wishfort, for example, in *The Way of the World*, is humiliated in the same manner as Cathos and Madelon in *Les Précieuses Ridicules*, and the contrasting character Millamant is rewarded with the good fortune due to youth and beauty, but other lines of action in the play, though helping to fill out an unrivaled picture of high society, cannot be said to enforce any thesis. The truth is, Restoration dramatists had no profound convictions to enforce, and they knew their audiences had no interest whatever in theses. After taking account of a few class prejudices and preferences, the playwright had no care but to keep his scene filled with moving figures. It was therefore impossible that he should employ Molière's method of constructing a plot on a controlling idea around a dominating character.

In connection with plot-structure we should consider the everlasting question of the unities. It is a familiar story that the rules which in the sixteenth century had been developed in Italy from the revival and misunderstanding of Aristotle, were in the seventeenth century in France enacted into criminal statutes. Molière, writing in the third quarter of the century, when the reign of classicism was most nearly absolute, observed the unities, not from fear of rigorous judges, but as a matter of convention. In *Don Juan* he threw them to the winds, and in the beginning of his career he used the Italian setting, so that a good many intimate conversations are held in the open street, — which seems to us a ridiculous place for such intimacies, but which seemed natural enough to his audience, — but in his comedies of character he observed the rules with as much ease as Racine. These rules were at the Restoration introduced into England along with French fans, coaches, and cheese. Indeed, the wits of the period looked back with a very complacent air of

superiority on the unpolished and even bar-
barous Elizabethans. The critical writings
of Dryden in particular exemplify this worship of regularity, though his sturdy English
nature caused some wavering in his ad-
herence to French leadership. In his own
practice and that of the period the influence
of the classical attitude was pervasive. No
matter how many lines of action a playwright
introduced, he placed all of them in the same
vicinity and concluded them in as short a
time as he conveniently could. The observ-
ance of unity of place was of course immensely
assisted by the introduction of painted scenery,
but that of unity of time must be ascribed
to the force of classicism alone.

Molière's part in this change in English
comedy was that of furnishing a model.
It is much easier to follow a rule when you
see how some one else has followed it. Shadwell gives clear testimony on this point in the
preface to his first production. He says: —

I have in this Play, as near as I could, observ'd the
three Unities, of Time, Place, and Action; The Time
of the Drama does not exceed six Hours, the Place is
in a very narrow Compass, and the main Action of the

Play, upon which all the rest depend, is the sullen Love betwixt Stanford and Emilia, which kind of Love is only proper to their Characters : I have here, as often as I could naturally, kept the Scenes unbroken, which (though it be not so much practis'd, or so well understood, by the English) yet among the French Poets is accounted a great Beauty.[1]

The particular French play he has in mind is of course *Le Misanthrope*, from which is taken a good part of the design, but he falls short of the success Molière attained in that drama. He brings in two minor intrigues which destroy the unity of action ;[2] he changes the scene twice within the act ;[3] and even in the unity of time he commits himself to the absurdity that two such characters as Stanford and Emilia would fall in love with each other and decide to marry within six hours after the first meeting.   Still, it is clear that Shadwell does his best to satisfy these unities, and that he does this in imitation of Molière. This first play is representative of his efforts to the close of his dramatic career ; what he tried to accomplish in *The Sullen Lovers*

[1] Shadwell, *Works*, i. 8.

[2] The Lovel-Carolina and the Positive-Vaine intrigues.

[3] In acts iii and v.

under the stimulus of *Le Misanthrope* he continued to strive for in *Epsom Wells, The Virtuoso*, and all his other original plays down to *The Volunteers*.

The influence of Molière on Etheredge in this matter is equally clear. In his first play he produced a tragi-comedy in which the comic plot was made up of three actions loosely connected. He also changed the scene twenty-six times, and thereby kept the mind of the spectator jumping about in anything but a restful fashion. The management was consequently as "rude and unpolished" as that of any Elizabethan drama. In the four years intervening before his second play, discussion of the French unities had become rife among the court wits, and Etheredge considered more carefully the method of Molière, the only French dramatist he appears to have known well. *She Would if She Could* accordingly had only three lines of action, all dexterously interwoven, and the scene was shifted only ten times. *Sir Fopling Flutter*, with only eleven shifts of scene, indicates the same attempt to observe the rules so far as the English demand for multiplicity of persons and liveliness of action would permit.

Of the period as a whole it may be said that, with all this classicism, the English did not study Molière as a master of construction, as so many modern dramatists have studied Ibsen for dramaturgic hints. These writers of comedy rather found in Molière the most familiar exemplification of the classical requirements they had already come to feel more or less constrained to observe.

Bound up with Molière's treatment of plot as a whole is his treatment of what is technically known as the exposition of the play. His openings are frequently masterpieces. The monologue of Argan in *Le Malade Imaginaire* gives us at once a complete understanding of the theme of the piece. In *Le Tartuffe* the quarrel of Madame Pernelle with her daughter-in-law not only reveals the situations upon which the whole plot depends, but is as genuinely comic as any scene in his theater. Such means of arousing interest and putting the audience in possession of the facts necessary to an understanding of the play were not very well adapted to plots where the attention was centered on incident rather than character, and as a matter of fact very few English dramatists spent much thought on Molière's devices. Congreve, a close student of all sides of Molière's art, opened *The Double Dealer* and *The Way of the World* with a conversation between the hero and his confidant in imitation of *Le Misanthrope*. In *Love for Love* the hero and his servant open the play, as in *Le Dépit Amoureux* and several of the lighter pieces of Molière. In *The Old Bachelor* and *The Way of the World* Congreve kept the spectators in suspense by deferring the entrance of the women till the second act, as French audiences had been kept waiting for the appearance of Célimène. Long before this Etheredge had focused attention on a central character by following the device employed in *Le Tartuffe*, that of not bringing the central character on the stage till the beginning of the third act. Crowne imitated Etheredge in this and other details in *Sir Courtly Nice*. But all such instances of imitation are isolated. There was no general tendency to study Molière's methods of exposition.

Le Tartuffe suggests a feature of Molière's expositions which resulted from his absorbing interest in character. In all his great comedies the introduction takes up the better part of two acts. The great care taken to prepare for the appearance of the arch-hypocrite Tartuffe is typical. In *L'École des Femmes*, for instance, we have reached the end of the second act before we are put in possession of the events that have taken place before the opening of the play. In *Le Misanthrope*, again, we must wait until near the end of the second act to become acquainted with all the characters and the relations existing among them. A glance at *The Country Wife* or *The Plain Dealer* will show that the same is largely true of Wycherley — a good part of the second act is with him given over to exposition. One reason is that he was borrowing another man's plots, so that it was not convenient to avoid this feature of Molière's development of the stratagem. Another reason is that there was an indirect influence. Wycherley, who had caught the idea from Molière's plays, was centering his attention on social criticism, so that his exposition naturally extended to a greater length than in the contemporary English comedy, whose plot-structure he was in the main following. The case of Congreve was somewhat different. He had in mind models for his different plays, but he followed them at a great distance. It is nevertheless true that the first two acts of all his plays but *The Old Bachelor* were largely given over to exposition, and consequently had the same lack of movement to be found in Molière. In Restoration comedy as a whole such length of exposition was rare, for it was perilous in the hands of any but a master. The Restoration playgoer would begin a conversation with his neighbor if there was not something interesting going on on the stage.

Another result of Molière's absorbing interest in character was the constant introduction of scenes which neither hinder nor hasten the *dénouement*. In one respect *Les Fâcheux* is typical of his whole method — the intrigue serves no purpose but to bring on the scene a musician, a pedant, a gamester, or a hunter ; that is, to display character. Plot was for him the frame for the portrait of a group against a background of manners.

One need dip into very few plays to justify the statement. In *L'Avare* the scene where the miser begins preparations for the dinner does not arouse any suspense concerning the outcome of the plot, but it is an intensely comic revelation of Harpagon's skinflint disposition. In *Les Femmes Savantes* the meeting of the learned ladies where Trissotin and Vadius revel in their pedantry is not introduced to disillusion Philaminte, as Scribe would have used it, but to give a brightly colored picture of the affectation Molière was attacking. In *Le Misanthrope* the scene where Alceste at length gives his opinion of the sonnet, and the other where Célimène expresses her estimate of the different persons of her acquaintance, are developed far beyond the requirements of the intrigue, but those conversations give a masterly delineation of the misanthrope and the coquette, and, moreover, carry out the satirical purpose for which the play was written. Throughout his comedy of manners Molière constantly followed this method, — sought the comic in the relation of the scene to life rather than in its relation to plot.

This feature of Molière's art the leading Restoration dramatists seized on with avidity. Etheredge in his first play gave several such pictures from the life of a gallant, but the following passage is handled with a lighter touch. Note that his delight in transcribing life caused him to linger over the scene much longer than was justified by its part in the plot.

THE NEW EXCHANGE. MRS.TRINKET *sitting in a shop: People passing by as in the Exchange.*

Trink. What d'ye buy? what d'ye lack, gentlemen? gloves, ribbons, and essences; ribbons, gloves, and essences?

Enter MR. COURTAL.

Mr. Courtal! I thought you had a quarrel to the Change, and were resolved we should never see you here again.

Court. Your unkindness indeed, Mrs. Trinket, had been enough to make a man banish himself forever.

Enter MRS. GAZETTE.

Trink. Look you, yonder comes fine Mrs. Gazette; thither you intend your visit, I am sure.

Gaz. Mr. Courtal! Your servant.

Court. Your servant, Mistress Gazette.

Gaz. This happiness was only meant to Mistress

Trinket ; had it not been my good fortune to pass by
by chance, I should have lost my share on't.

Court. This is too cruel, Mistress Gazette, when all
the unkindness is on your side, to rally your servant thus.

Gaz. I vow this tedious absence of yours made me
believe you intended to try an experiment on my poor
heart, to discover that hidden secret, how long a despair-
ing lover may languish without the sight of the party.

Court. You are always very pleasant on this subject,
Mistress Gazette.

Gaz. And have not you reason to be so?

Court. Not that I know of.

Gaz. Yes, you hear the good news.

Court. What good news?

Gaz. How well this dissembling becomes you !
But now I think better on't, it cannot concern you ;
you are more a gentleman than to have an amour last
longer than an Easter term with a country lady ; and
yet there are some, I see, as well in the country as in
the city, that have a pretty way of huswifing a lover,
and can spin an intrigue out a great deal farther than
others are willing to do. . . . [She shows she knows
Courtal's relations to Lady Cockwood.] I have furnished her and the young ladies with a few fashionable
toys since they came to town, to keep 'em in countenance
at a play or in the Park.

Court. I would have thee go immediately to the young
ladies, and by some device or other entice 'em hither.

Gaz. I came just now from taking measure of 'em
for a couple of handkerchiefs.

Court. How unlucky's this !

Gaz. They are calling for their hoods and scarves, and are coming hither to lay out a little money in ribbons and essences. I have recommended them to Mistress Trinket's shop here. . . .

Court. [*to Freeman*]. Leave all things to me, and hope the best. Begone, for I expect their coming immediately ; walk a turn or two above, or fool awhile with pretty Mistress Anvil, and scent your eyebrows and periwig with a little essence of oranges or jessamine ; and when you see us all together at Mistress Gazette's shop, put in as it were by chance.[1]

Wycherley had the same interest in life, but he drew with heavier lines and painted with deeper colors. His first play illustrates the satirical bent of his nature.

Mrs. Crossbite's *Dining-room.* *Enter* Dapperwit *and* Ranger.

Ran. But she will not hear you ; she's as deaf as if you were a dun or a constable.

Dap. Pish ! give her but leave to gape, rub her eyes, and put on her day pinner ; the long patch under the left eye ; awaken the roses on her cheeks with some Spanish wool, and warrant her breath with some lemon-peel ; the doors fly off the hinges, and she into my arms. She knows there is as much artifice to keep a victory

[1] *She Would if She Could*, iii. 1 (p. 157 ff.).

as to gain it ; and 'tis a sign she values the conquest of my heart.

Ran. I thought her beauty had not stood in need of art.

Dap. Beauty's a coward still without the help of art, and may have the fortune of a conquest but cannot keep it. Beauty and art can no more be asunder than love and honour.

Ran. Or, to speak more like yourself, wit and judgment.

Dap. Don't you hear the door wag yet?

Ran. Not a whit.

Dap. Miss ! miss ! 'tis your slave that calls. Come, all this tricking for him ! — Lend me your comb, Mr. Ranger.

Ran. No, I am to be preferred to-day, you are to set me off. You are in possession, I will not lend you arms to keep me out.

Dap. A pox ! don't let me be ungrateful ; if she has smugged herself up for me, let me prune and flounce my peruke a little for her. There's ne'er a young fellow in the town but will do as much for a mere stranger in the playhouse.

Ran. A wit's wig has the privilege of being uncombed in the very playhouse, or in the presence.

Dap. But not in the presence of his mistress ; 'tis a greater neglect of her than himself. Pray lend me your comb.

Ran. I would not have men of wit and courage make use of every fop's mean arts to keep or gain a mistress.

Dap. But don't you see every day, though a man have never so much wit and courage, his mistress will revolt to those fops that wear and comb perukes well. I'll break off the bargain, and will not receive you my partner.

Ran. Therefore you see I am setting up for myself. [*Combs his peruke.*][1]

But Wycherley frequently took very little pains to relate his cutting observations on the manners and customs of his time to the character uttering them. In adapting *Le Misanthrope*, for example, he went far beyond the original satire. In the second act of *The Plain Dealer* he reproduced the scandal scene of the French play with entirely superfluous additions that expanded it to more than twice its original length. In much the same manner the third act of the English comedy was devoted to satirical remarks on law and the practices of lawyers. Indeed, a distinguishing characteristic of Wycherley's comedy as a whole was the attention paid to witty realism, no matter how little it might contribute to the story or the delineation of character.

[1] *Love in a Wood*, iii. 2 (p. 61 f.).

Etheredge and Wycherley, it will be remembered, got their first notion of Molière's comedy of manners from *Les Précieuses Ridicules*, where most of the piece is filled with conversation that serves only to ridicule the cult of preciosity. That was what the play existed for. There was only so much plot as was necessary to effect that purpose. Congreve was not only a greater artist than his predecessors in England, but he had the advantage of studying Molière's masterpieces from the start, so that his satirical passages were handled more skilfully than those of Wycherley and Etheredge. His love of wordplay, to be sure, led him to endow his minor characters, the servants in particular, with too much brilliant wit, but in general his satire, frequently as it might suspend the action, had some more or less obvious relation to character and purpose. Indeed, his copy of the scene from *Le Misanthrope* just referred to was managed better even than in the original, for while in Molière the other persons merely furnished suggestions for the sharpness of Célimène's wit, in Congreve there was a give and take in the dialogue that was more dramatic. A better illustration of the thoroughness with which Congreve learned his lesson may be found in *Love for Love*, where Valentine is trying to secure his inheritance from his father. This should be compared with the scene in *L'Avaro* where Maître Simon, who has been acting as agent for the father, Harpagon, in putting money out to usury, and for the son, Cléante, in trying to effect a loan, brings the two together without knowing their relationship. A single reading shows that the conversation in the two passages is managed in the same way.[1] Each scene lights up the character of father and son, advances the action a little, and is at the same time a keen satire on miserliness.

The method of Etheredge and Wycherley, however, was the one followed by the vast majority of Restoration playwrights. In this matter the influence of Molière was far more pervasive than in the features of his structure previously considered. There was hardly a man who would not pause in the busiest intrigue to limn a sketch from Covent Garden

[1] Cf. *Love for Love*, ii. 1 (p. 228 ff.), and *L'Avare*, ii. 2.

or some popular tavern. For it was no secret
that a playgoer's attention could frequently be
caught sooner by a scene which he recognized
or thought he recognized than by the greatest
briskness of movement.

A third and last result of Molière's centering his interest on character more than on
plot was the kind of solutions he found for
his intrigues. In *Les Femmes Savantes* the
impossible suitor is frightened away by a pretended loss of wealth. *Le Tartuffe* is ended
by the intervention of the King. In *L'Avare*
a long-lost father returns to lead the loving
pairs into each other's arms. Molière was
almost obliged to bring about the conclusion
by such extraneous means, because his characters were always fixed types, men who were
subject to no gradual development or great
moral revolution. There is nothing more
characteristic of Harpagon than his conduct
in the last scene of *L'Avare*. There is no
possible ending to the schemes of Tartuffe
so satisfying to our emotions or so appropriate
to the characters as the one Molière has
devised. The fault with his *dénouements* is
not that they are inconsistent with the play,

but that they are not always carefully evolved from its inner structure.

English dramatists noticed this feature of Molière's plots, but they naturally regarded it as a fault. I have already shown how Medbourne in his translation prepared for the overthrow of Tartuffe by the introduction of a legal document. Crowne, who adapted the main features of the French play, deferred the unmasking scene to the last act and utilized it to bring about the conclusion. But the *dénouement* of most plays of the period is of the intrigue type, where the misunderstandings and cases of mistaken identity are all explained, for such endings were necessary to clear up the confusions of the plot.

This survey makes it clear that Molière had a very slight influence on the plot-structure of Restoration comedy. The English dramatists were not profound and penetrating psychologists, so that his methods were entirely out of keeping with their aims. The only pervasive influence was the tendency to interrupt the movement in order to linger over scenes from contemporary life, and that influence was not the result of direct imita-

tion, but of the interest Molière had started
in the recognition of scenes from daily life
as a source of popular appeal. The smallness
of the influence on structure is entirely explained by the facts given in the last chapter on the general attitude toward Molière.
Even in composing comedies of intrigue the
playwrights did not study the Frenchman's
lighter work. These men were not eager
and fastidious artists cherishing lofty ideals
for the drama and poring over the greatest
models in hope of attaining some far-off
perfection. They were practical playwrights
working for the approval of a narrow coterie
or the commercial reward of popular success.
They did the practical thing of trying their
best to please their audience, and they were
in no doubt concerning the tastes of that
audience. One of the characters in Etheredge is given a remark that explains both the
life and the drama of the period :—

A single intrigue in love is as dull as a single plot in
a play, and will tire a lover worse than t'other does an
audience.[1]

[1] *She Would if She Could*, iii. 1 (p. 161).

CHAPTER VI

CHARACTER

THE demand of Restoration audiences for several lines of action is to some extent explained by the prevailing interest in variety of character. Seeing nothing but the superficial side of life, those audiences got tired of watching the same persons come upon the stage time and again. The playwrights found it much easier to borrow characters than to invent them, and they discovered that Molière was one of the most convenient sources for borrowings. A great deal of this adaptation was made with no attempt to preserve the spirit of the original. I need not advert to the treatment of character in Lacy or Ravenscroft. The ordinary treatment of Molière's conceptions may be observed in Shadwell's *Bury Fair*, the main stratagem and chief characters of which were taken from *Les Précieuses Ridicules*. Wildish, a fine gentleman from London who has come to Bury to seek his beloved, conceives the idea of passing off his peruke-maker as a count on two rustic blue-stockings, Lady Fantast and her daughter, not because he has been rejected as a lover, but because their affectation disgusts him.[1] This pretended count in his conversation makes reference to army experiences,[2] as Mascarille and Jodelet do ; he has the ladies try the scent of his powdered peruke,[3] as Mascarille does ; and at one point he is cudgeled [4] as the French servants are. That is pretty close imitation of externals, but none of the peruke-maker's dialogue with Lady Fantast and her daughter, though fully as affected as that of the French valets, is translated or paraphrased from Molière. As La Roche is a copy of Mascarille and Jodelet, so Lady Fantast and her daughter, Mrs. Fantast, are copies of Madelon and Cathos, but their special affectation is the French lan-

[1] *Bury Fair*, i (pp. 137–139). Cf. *Les Précieuses Ridicules*, sc. 1.

[2] *Ibid.*, ii (p. 155). Cf. *Les Précieuses Ridicules*, sc. 11.

[3] *Ibid.*, iii (p. 180). Cf. *Les Précieuses Ridicules*, sc. 9.

[4] *Ibid.*, iv (p. 195 f.). Cf. *Les Précieuses Ridicules*, sc. 13.

guage rather than heroic romances. This element of the original satire is preserved, however, in the conversation of the country fop,
Trim, with Mrs. Fantast, in which they display their reading of heroic romances by ad-
dressing each other as Dorinda and Eugenius.
Compared with Molière these figures are lacking in comic force, but judged by the work of
contemporary playwrights the satire is found
to be much better adapted to English conditions, and the figures accordingly more appropriate in an English drama, than was usually
the case with such borrowing.

There was, however, another class of borrowed characters in which a good deal of the
spirit of Molière was preserved. One of the
most famous figures in all Restoration comedy
is an instance. Sir Fopling Flutter is the
most airily graceful of Restoration fops, has
the most delightfully fastidious taste and the
most affected fine manners. He owes these
qualities not solely to the lightness and gaiety
of Sir George Etheredge himself. He owes
them in no slight degree to the Mascarille of
Les Précieuses Ridicules. Certainly the author after having seen Molière in this rôle

in Paris could never forget the experience.
It was perfectly natural, therefore, that Etheredge should transfer the character to one
of his own comedies when social conditions
had developed a similar degree of foppery in
England. So much of the original was retained in the transference that one can be
in no doubt concerning the method. Fopling's
attempt to dance [1] and his later attempt to
sing [2] were clearly in imitation of Mascarille's
vanity,[3] but the most suggestive passage is
one exhibiting his finical attention to matters
of dress.

[LADY TOWNLEY, EMILIA, MR. MEDLEY, DORIMANT,
SIR FOPLING FLUTTER.]

Lady Town. He's very fine.

Emil. Extreme proper.

Sir Fop. A slight suit I made to appear in at my
first arrival, not worthy your consideration, ladies.

Dor. The pantaloon is very well mounted.

Sir Fop. The tassels are new and pretty.

Med. I never saw a coat better cut.

Sir Fop. It makes me show long-waisted, and, I
think, slender.

[1] *Sir Fopling Flutter*, iv. 1 (p. 327).
[2] *Ibid.*, iv. 2 (p. 338).
[3] *Les Précieuses Ridicules*, sc. 9.

Dor. That's the shape our ladies dote on.

Med. Your breech, though, is a handful too high in my eye, Sir Fopling.

Sir Fop. Peace, Medley; I have wished it lower a thousand times, but a pox on't, 'twill not be.

Lady Town. His gloves are well fringed, large and graceful.

Sir Fop. I always was eminent for being *bien-ganté*.

Emil. He wears nothing but what are originals of the most famous hands in Paris.

Sir Fop. You are in the right, madam.

Lady Town. The suit?

Sir Fop. Barroy.

Emil. The garniture?

Sir Fop. Le Gras.

Med. The shoes?

Sir Fop. Piccat.

Dor. The periwig?

Sir Fop. Chedreux.

Lady Town. and Emil. The gloves?

Sir Fop. Orangerie: you know the smell, ladies. Dorimant, I could find in my heart for an amusement to have a gallantry with some of our English ladies.[1]

[MAGDELON, CATHOS, MASCARILLE.]

Mas. Que vous semble de ma petite-oie? La trouvez-vous congruante à l'habit?

Cath. Tout à fait.

Mas. Le ruban est bien choisi.

[1] *Sir Fopling Flutter*, iii. 2 (p. 297 f.).

Mag. Furieusement bien. C'est Perdrigeon tout pur.

Mas. Que dites-vous de mes canons?

Mag. Ils ont tout à fait bon air.

Mas. Je puis me vanter au moins qu'ils ont un grand quartier plus que tous ceux qu'on fait.

Mag. Il faut avouer que je n'ai jamais vu porter si haut l'élégance de l'ajustement.

Mas. Attachez un peu sur ces gants la réflexion de votre odorat.

Mag. Ils sentent terriblement bon.

Cath. Je n'ai jamais respiré une odeur mieux conditionnée.

Mas. Et celle-là? [*Il donne à sentir les cheveux poudrés de sa perruque.*]

Mag. Elle est tout à fait de qualité; le sublime en est touché délicieusement.

Mas. Vous ne me dites rien de mes plumes: comment les trouvez-vous?

Cath. Effroyablement belles.

Mas. Savez-vous que le brin me coûte un louis d'or? Pour moi, j'ai cette manie de vouloir donner généralement sur tout ce qu'il y a de plus beau.

Mag. Je vous assure que nous sympathisons vous et moi: j'ai une délicatesse furieuse pour tout ce que je porte; et jusqu'à mes chaussettes, je ne puis rien souffrir qui ne soit de la bonne ouvrière.[1]

Obvious as the borrowing is, the adaptation was so complete that the audience

[1] *Les Précieuses Ridicules*, sc. 9.

thought they recognized in more than one
dandy of the courtly circle the original for
Etheredge's conception.[1] The figure was, in
fact, so good a reflection of contemporary life
that Crowne and Cibber and Vanbrugh, to
mention the most noteworthy imitators,
helped to make it one of the most pleasant
and characteristic comic types of the period.
They failed to attain the lightness and grace
of Etheredge's adaptation, partly because
they had never absorbed the comic spirit of
the Frenchman. For adaptations of this
kind, one hardly need remark, were possible
only to men who could in a degree assume
Molière's attitude of never-tiring delicate
ridicule toward all things unreasonable.

The consideration of these borrowings —
both of the extremely small class which retained a good deal of Molière's spirit and of
the extremely large class in which little attention was paid to the integrity or the particular effectiveness of the original — does not
exhaust the question of influence. For such
borrowings might be made quite independently of any adoption of Molière's peculiar

[1] Cf. Etheredge, p. xiv, note 1.

methods of character-drawing. The author of *Le Misanthrope*, to be sure, was not a devoted student of dramaturgic devices nor a clever exploiter of technical resources. But he spent considerable thought on the grouping and contrasting of his characters, not only to heighten dramatic effectiveness, but also to emphasize the idea upon which each play was based. In praising his friend, Mignard, he noted that painter's noble arrangement of contrasted groups,[1] a feature of painting not suggested by Du Fresnoy, the source of several of his opinions.[2] In his dramas he made notable use of contrast from the beginning. In *Le Dépit Amoureux*, for instance, he employed the frequent Spanish device for heightening comic effect by presenting the love affairs of a servant as a foil to those of the master. In *L'École des Maris* he opposed the severe Sganarelle to the indulgent Ariste, not only for clearer portrayal of character, but to make the thesis of the play more prominent. Indeed, take any of Molière's pieces that comes to hand, and you will find

[1] Cf. *La Gloire du Val-de-grâce*, l. 74.
[2] Cf. Molière, *Œuvres*, ix. 518 ff., 540.

contrast utilized to render the comedy more effective, the characters more striking, and the idea of the play more unmistakable.

The skill with which Molière employed the device is so considerable that it would have been very strange if the Restoration dramatists who thought him anything but a storehouse of incidents had not seen it. But it is quite another matter to be able to trace his influence on so common a practice. Dryden, with his keen and powerful intellect and his small native aptitude for the theater, paid more attention to technical matters than most playwrights of the time. In *Limberham*, for example, he arranged the characters in a very symmetrical pattern. Aldo, the openhearted befriender of mistresses, is set over against Mrs. Saintly, the hypocritical keeper of a "boarding-house"; Brainsick, despising his wife, against Limberham, doting on his mistress; the wheedling Mrs. Brainsick against the termagant Mrs. Tricksy; Aldo's son, Woodall, a rake, against Mrs. Saintly's supposed daughter, the virtuous Pleasance; even the servant Gervase, giving his master good counsel, against the maid Judith, obeying strictly her mistress's behests. Giles is the only unbalanced character in the whole play, and he is used merely to untie the knot at the close. Of course this is all very pretty in its geometrical regularity, but it affords no evidence of influence from Molière's vital contrasts.

Crowne was likewise too careful a workman to neglect the principle. In *Sir Courtly Nice* he made notable use of it to introduce satirical realism into the Spanish plot he was adapting. Hothead and Testimony, representing the royalist and Presbyterian parties, are brought into continual altercation, in which the heat of the one and the affected calmness of the other present a very amusing spectacle. Even more effective is the contrast between the exquisite, super-refined Sir Courtly and the coarse, rude Surly. One feels that Crowne, a student of Molière's characters, was under his influence in thus making contrast serve his satirical purpose as well as the heightening of comic effect. In the case of Wycherley imitation is as certain as such matters can be. He not only made his contrasts sharp and complete, but in giving the persons opposing

views of life he contrived to enforce the more
or less definite thesis of his play. The vehemence of his temperament and the well-
recognized tastes of an English audience combined to rob his contrasts of restraint, but
the result in every case gives one the impression that the brilliant Englishman was merely
trying to improve on the methods of Molière.
The dissimilarity between such rôles as the
ridiculously jealous Pinchwife and the ridiculously trustful Sparkish, or the excessively
rough Manly and the excessively complaisant
Plausible, even though less natural than that
between Sganarelle and Ariste, was, I feel
sure, drawn in imitation of the French master.
I hardly need add that such a statement can
be made of very few dramatists of the period.

In the drawing of individual character
Molière displayed peculiarities that may at
first puzzle an English reader. At any rate,
the coloring he gave to his *dramatis personæ*
was misunderstood by such a considerable
critic as Hazlitt.[1] Molière, however, knew
exactly what he was about. He was not a
literary student poring over dramatic master-

[1] Cf. Hazlitt, *Works*, viii. 28 f.

pieces in an endeavor to emulate the poetic beauties of the classics. He was an actor, probably the greatest comic actor of his time. He was stage-manager and producer and advertiser of all the plays brought out by his company. He therefore was perfectly familiar with the demands of presentation in a theater. He knew that the playgoer has no time to study out the subtle significance of a trait of character or the esoteric meaning of a polished speech. He knew, moreover, that to be impressive character and incidents cannot be presented in the humdrum manner of everyday life. Recently a student who was serving as supernumerary in a famous opera performed in New York City, stood behind the scenes to watch one of the best actors on the operatic stage. "He was painted like a savage and grinned like an idiot," the student declared afterward. But that coloring and that grimace impressed on the audience the anguish of a tragic moment when the music was yearning like a god in pain. So Molière in his character-drawing, in order to impress on the audience his conception of a person, exaggerated traits beyond what would be manifested on the street or in the home. This principle accounts for the almost farcical coloring given to Harpagon in *L'Avare*. The miser is so much interested in his search for valuables on the person of a servant that he demands to see still other hands after La Flèche has already shown both right and left.[1] At the end of the act he exclaims with delight, after listening to a declaration that money is more precious than youth, beauty, birth, wisdom, or uprightness : "Ah, what a fine fellow! That was spoken like an oracle. Happy is the man with a servant of that kind!"[2] The same method is employed in his most serious and realistic delineations. Tartuffe enters on the scene for the first time giving directions to his servant : "Laurent, put away my hair shirt and my scourge, and pray that heaven may always light your pathway. If any one calls for me, say that I am visiting the prisoners to share with them what little alms I have received."[3]

[1] *L'Avare*, i. 3.
[2] *Ibid.*, i. 5.
[3] *Le Tartuffe*, iii. 2.

This footlight shading is a conspicuous feature of Molière's character-drawing, but it is no more distinctive of his art than the use of contrast. Every playwright who has any practical knowledge of theatrical requirements finds such coloring necessary. The presence of dramatic heightening in Restoration comedy is nevertheless in many cases to be ascribed to the influence of Molière, because the borrowing of his characters was frequent, and it was much harder to keep from observing his method in individual delineations than in the arrangement of groups. Two illustrations will suffice. Crowne constantly employed it in a way to remind one of the French genius. Sir Thomas Rash in *The Country Wit* makes statements like the following threat to his daughter : —

Sir Mannerly will be in town to-morrow, and to-morrow he shall marry you before he sleeps, nay, before his boots are off, nay, before he lights off his horse ; he shall marry you a horse-back but he shall marry you to-morrow.[1]

One immediately recalls Orgon's infatuation for the hypocrite : —

[1] *The Country Wit*, i. (p. 20).

Il m'enseigne à n'avoir affection pour rien,
De toutes amitiés il détache mon âme ;
Et je verrois mourir frère, enfants, mère et femme,
Que je m'en soucierois autant que de cela.[1]

Other passages, such as the speeches of Lord Stately in *The English Friar*, or of Sir Courtly in *Sir Courtly Nice*, contain the same kind of exaggeration that Molière adopted to bring his figures into proper perspective before an audience.

In Wycherley, too, the influence is obvious. In *Love in a Wood* Mrs. Crossbite praises Dapperwit to the procuress, Mrs. Joyner, but as soon as the latter proposes a better "keeper" for her daughter Lucy, she exclaims : "D'ye hear, daughter, Mrs. Joyner has satisfied me clearly ; Dapperwit is a vile fellow, and, in short, you must put an end to that scandalous familiarity between you."[2] It is the voice of Géronte, who, when he learns that Léandre has inherited a large fortune, suddenly desists from his violent opposition : "Monsieur, votre vertu m'est tout à fait considérable, et je vous donne ma fille avec

[1] *Le Tartuffe*, i. 5.
[2] *Love in a Wood*, iii. 1 (p. 57).

la plus grande joie du monde." [1] Numerous little touches like this show that Wycherley in his exaggerations was imitating the method of Molière. But in this matter as much as in the use of contrast the Englishman thought it necessary to improve on his model. Olivia in *The Plain Dealer,* though borrowed from *Le Misanthrope,* is portrayed too glaringly to win any credence. The affectation of Paris or Don Diego in *The Gentleman Dancing Master* is presented with so much exaggeration that neither of them is convincing. Indeed, all his leading persons are delineated with so little restraint that they give an impression of unreality not in keeping with the plays as wholes.

A second characteristic of Molière's delineations is that he never traces the development or unfolding of character. Even the dominating personalities in his most serious plays never change from the first scene to the last. Alceste after his rejection by Célimène remains the same champion of high ideals in conflict with the hypocritical society about him that he was in the open-

[1] *Le Médecin malgré lui,* iii. 11.

ing of the play in conversation with Oronte.
The different scenes where he appears merely
throw brighter light upon one or another
phase of his character. In a word, Molière's
characters are static. This is quite different
from the method familiar to English students
in Shakspere. Shakspere traces the development of ambition in the soul of Macbeth
and the resulting deterioration of character,
or the gradual awakening of jealousy in the
mind of Othello and the terrible and pitiful
consequences thereof. What Shakspere was
interested in was the biography of a soul.
His prevailing method was to study evolution,
degeneration, change.

One explanation of the difference is that
Molière was writing comedy. I think I have
already made it clear that pure comedy is
impossible wherever sympathy is aroused.
Now intense sympathy is aroused by the
spectacle of a soul's development. It is only
static figures, where incongruities are salient,
that are genuinely and consistently comic.
Shakspere illustrates this as well as Molière.
No Elizabethan audience ever found development in Touchstone or Bottom or

Dogberry. Unlike Shakspere, Molière was always and everywhere following the methods of comedy. Even his most somber, sinister figure is not presented as tragic. Tartuffe, it is true, does not raise much laughter; he is not a strictly comic figure, but it would be a total misunderstanding of the play to suppose that he was intended to arouse tragic interest.

A further explanation of why Molière's figures are characterized by a lack of development is that he makes them typical, general; he founds them upon an idea. Shakspere's are strictly individual and have general significance only because they are true to universal laws of being. But Molière, it will be remembered, was writing in an age and country far different from Elizabethan England. I need not repeat what I have previously said about the strong spirit of society which permeated the Paris of Louis XIV. I need not insist, either, on the strong classical ideals which dominated the literary circles of that time and found their most complete exemplification in the drama. Every one understands that ancient models

and the new unities were equally hostile to
Shakspere's biographic interest in character.
French society was certainly in complete
contrast with the worship of individualism
that saturated the London of Elizabeth and
with the spirit of revolt from all classic con-
straints that animated the young poets of
her reign. The French spirit of society and
classicism and the English love of the individual and the irregular could not but get
themselves expressed in the drama of the two
periods. But more important for Molière's
character drawing was the influence of the
commedia dell' arte. The masks of the Italians,
though realistic enough in their origin, were for
the French nothing but general types vivified
by the histrionic genius of successive actors.
Molière's servants and lovers and old men
were at first merely brilliant specimens of
the Italian mask. That is, he formed his
method of character-drawing by imitation
of general types, and that method, gradually
modified by his developing genius, he
employed throughout his career. But the
method was peculiarly suited to his temperament. I have already emphasized the clarity

of his thinking, the dominance of reason over fancy in his sense of comedy, the submission of all details to a controlling idea in his construction of plot. The same mental attitude determined his character-drawing. His characters were founded on an idea. Harpagon presents many a facet of avarice. Tartuffe has become the synonym for hypocrisy. *Le Misanthrope* has been considered a modern form of the medieval "morality" with its group of personified abstractions. This is a very grievous exaggeration, to be sure, but it illustrates an essential difference between Molière and Shakspere. Molière has all the interest in general ideas and the love of lucidity characteristic of the French. Shakspere was interested in searching out the secrets of personality and exploring all the mysterious corners of the individual soul. His creations have the complexity of life, and are often more baffling than any of our acquaintances. Molière presented a simplified transcript from life. His characters revealed the dominance of an idea connected with the theme upon which the play was based.

Molière's method of character-drawing suggests Ben Jonson's theory of humors. Both men adopted an intellectual simplification of life, as opposed to the rich imaginative imitation to be found in Shakspere. Jonson, like Molière, centered his interest on the dominating characteristic of each person. In late life, to be sure, he carried the method to a bare and lifeless allegory, but in his best work he produced figures, such as Bobadil, that must have been as convincing on the stage as the valiant Nym or mine ancient Pistol. Where, then, it may be asked, lies the difference between Jonson and Molière? The difference is not so much in the method of presenting character as in the men who used the method. Jonson surely had a strong intellect and a gift for shrewd observation. He filled out his conceptions with all the realism necessary for rendering the characters convincing behind the footlights. But when subjected to the analysis of the study, the product remains rather thin in comparison not only with Shakspere, but with Molière. For Molière as well as Shakspere had a penetrating imagination. He, too, created characters that are individual, though he was at the same time careful to show them as typical. He presented the large, fat Tartuffe, with his florid complexion and enormous appetite and domineering manners. He delineated the passionately sincere Alceste, who yet has the urbanity of a courtier, and, by a stroke of genius which preserved some of the inconsistency of life, had him love the most elegantly coquettish mistress of a fashionable salon. Molière never devoted a play to the fate brooding over human life nor to the destiny that awaits man hereafter. He was interested in this world. But he had the gift of imagination to create characters as living, as human, as true to life as he saw it, as any in Shakspere. His peculiarity is that his imagination was always subject to the control of intellect, that in imitating life he always simplified so as to make his characters unmistakably typical.

This method of delineating static and typical characters based on an idea is intimately related to Molière's conception of comedy, which was that it should correct the follies and foibles of men, and particularly of the

men of his time.[1]   One might therefore expect
that the method would be adopted in England
only so far as the basic conception was shared
by the English playwrights.   A few concrete
comparisons will bear out the supposition.
The case of Wycherley, who did as much as
Etheredge to establish Molière's kind of
comedy in England, is typical.   In *L'École
des Femmes*, which we know he studied,
Arnolphe is a man who places ridiculous
emphasis on securing a faithful wife.   It is
the incongruity between his methods and the
dictates of reason that Molière makes the
source of all the comic effect he draws from
this character.   Every precaution he takes
to attain his object serves only to render him
ridiculous.   The servants he has selected as
best suited to protect the innocence of his intended wife are a source of untold annoyance;
the simplicity of Agnès, upon which he
chiefly relies, in a dozen ways helps to defeat
his aims ; and his own active efforts near
the close have no result but to secure Agnès
to her lover, Horace.   This method Wycherley followed only in part.   In *The Country*

[1] Cf. *Le Tartuffe : Préface, Premier Placet.*

Wife Pinchwife is an excessively jealous husband whose jealousy at every point brings on the fate he fights against. Yet even when Wycherley was using a suggestion from Molière he did not always restrict himself to this method of developing the character from some basal incongruity. Paris in *The Gentleman Dancing Master* is based on the Sganarelle of *L'École des Maris*. A good part of the comic effect is accordingly produced by the contradiction between what he thinks he is accomplishing and what he actually accomplishes : he thinks he is making his rival Gerrard utterly ridiculous when he is in reality making a complete fool of himself. But this is not the only source of humor in his character ; he also gives rise to laughter by his absurd aping of French manners. In his original characters Wycherley came no nearer the method. Sparkish in *The Country Wife*, for instance, has some resemblance to Paris ; he thinks he is a great wit when he is a perfect wittol. Still, this incongruity is not the only feature emphasized, for Sparkish is also made to serve as an antithesis to jealous Pinchwife. The use of such distracting additions is on

reflection seen to be the logical outcome of
the failure to adopt Molière's plot-structure :
since Wycherley introduced no central thesis
controlling all parts of the play, there was no
necessity for his developing each comic character from a basal incongruity related to
the central thesis He was free to combine
in a single rôle as many sources of comic
effect as he chose.

Dryden, who was led to a realization of
Molière's conception through the success of
Wycherley and Etheredge, after 1671 drew
characters in somewhat the same way. The
comic underplot of *Marriage à la Mode*, as
I have remarked before, showed that Dryden
had been studying Molière carefully. Not
only Melantha, a very clever adaptation,
but the original figures, Doralice and Rho-
dophil, were developed from a central incongruity, though it must be confessed the
characters do not all enforce the idea of the
sub-plot as a whole. In some plays it is a
minor action that embodies the satiric purpose. The character of Judge Gripus, the
third person in the Mercury-Phædra intrigue
in *Amphitryon*, was in all likelihood a satire on

well-known practices of the bench, and the
intrigue between the god and the maid could
have been paralleled in the society of the time.
Such killing of two birds with one stone was a
renunciation of Molière's method of variously
illustrating a central idea. It was therefore
only in part that Dryden employed Molière's
method of character development. He nowhere invented his action and depicted his
persons to explain or enforce a controlling
idea, and even in the delineation of individual
borrowed rôles he followed at a considerable
distance the master's development of a central
incongruity.

In this matter Crowne was a better workman. The plot of *The English Friar* was
adapted from *Le Tartuffe* in order to satirize
the power of the church under James II.
Crowne, of course, had no difficulty in fitting
the figures from that play into the demands
of the English satire, but when we find Harpagon from *L'Avare* appearing as Lady Pinchgut
we think the author has merely yielded to
the common English demand for many persons. He certainly reproduces the comic
incongruity of the original. Lady Pinchgut's

starving the servants,[1] keeping the liveries
under key except when needed for special
occasions,[2] reducing her horses to skeletons
by locking the oats up in her closet,[3] making
her household observe all the fasts of the
church [4] — all these revelations by the coach-
man are reminiscences or variations from
L'Avare.[5] The relations between master and
servants in the original, with railings on one
side and frequent impertinence on the other,
are also reproduced in the English imitation.
But Lady Pinchgut is introduced not merely
to lend variety to the *dramatis personæ*.
Crowne makes the rôle serve his purpose of
exposing the power of the priesthood as completely as he adapts the plot of *Le Tartuffe*
to the same purpose.

His case merely furnishes one more illustration of the general statement that it was
only in so far as a Restoration playwright
adopted Molière's conception of comedy

[1] *The English Friar*, p. 46.
[2] *Ibid.*, p. 45.
[3] *Ibid.*, p. 65.
[4] *Ibid.*, p. 113.
[5] In particular, cf. *L'Avare*, iii. 1, especially the speech
of Maître Jacques at the end of the scene.

that he followed the Frenchman's method of drawing character. In other words, the large class of dramatists who in borrowing conceptions paid little attention to the integrity or peculiar effectiveness of the original were not influenced by Molière's employment of contrast in the grouping of *dramatis personæ* and, in the delineation of individual persons, by his method of dramatic heightening and of developing typical figures, founded on an idea, to carry out the theme of a play as a whole. Such influence was felt only by the small class who sought to retain or reproduce the spirit of Molière's comedy.

CHAPTER VII

DIALOGUE

NOT only can audiences determine the kind of plots a dramatist shall construct and the types of character he shall present, but they can influence, not very deeply perhaps, but nevertheless unmistakably, the style of dialogue he shall write. For though style is rightly considered the expression of individual temperament, external features have always been introduced in accordance with the peculiar likes and dislikes of the playgoer. Such an external feature is the lubricity which has almost become synonymous with Restoration dialogue. Not only were the ephemeral playwrights willing to insert passages having no attraction but their indecency, but some of the most sparkling wit of the leaders played around subjects now no longer alluded to in refined society. I need dwell on this notorious characteristic no longer than I have on the delight in amorous intrigues. It is already indelibly stamped on every man's memory. Besides, it has absolutely nothing to do with Molière's influence.

There is, however, some very tangible evidence of his influence in the dialogue of the leading dramatists. A recurrent feature of his plays is the passages of lively staccato conversation which were possibly a reminiscence of the *lazzi* indulged in by the actors of the *commedia dell' arte*. Such passages are at any rate totally opposed to the love of reasoning and long speeches characteristic of French drama. Etheredge was apparently impressed by the gaiety and sprightliness of those conversations when vivified by the consummate acting of Molière in *Les Précieuses Ridicules*.[1] The opening of his first play bears witness to the impression.

[CLARK, *servant to* LORD BEAUFORT, *and* DUFOY, *French valet to* SIR FREDERICK, *are speaking.*]

    Clark. Good-morrow, monsieur.
    Duf. Good-mor', — good-mor'.
    Clark. Is Sir Frederick stirring?
    Duf. Pox sturré himé.

    [1] On Molière's acting, cf. Larroumet, p. 358 ff.

Clark. My lord has sent me —

Duf. Begar, me vil havé de revengé ; me vil no stay two day in Englandé.

Clark. Good monsieur, what's the matter?

Duf. De matré! de matré is easy to be perceive.[1]

Throughout the piece the device was repeated time and again.

[*The Bailiffs enter as* Sir Frederick, Sir Nicholas, *and* Wheedle *are talking.*]

Bailiffs. We arrest you, sir.

Wheed. Arrest me? Sir Frederick, Sir Nicholas!

Sir Fred. We are not provided for a rescue at present, sir.

Wheed. At whose suit?

Bailiffs. At Sir Frederick Frollick's.

Wheed. Sir Frederick Frollick's? I owe him never a farthing.

Sir Fred. You're mistaken, sir ; you owe me a thousand pounds.[2]

Staccato dialogue was in Molière frequently combined with repetition almost to the extent of becoming a mannerism. Possibly that fact explains why the feature crept into Congreve's dialogue, for he had an ideal of style directly opposed to Molière's. He nevertheless imitated this particular mannerism

[1] *Love in a Tub*, i. 1 (p. 7).
[2] *Ibid.*, v. 4 (p. 107).

in more than one passage. The similarities in the following excerpts render extended comment unnecessary.

[SCANDAL, FORESIGHT.]

Scan. You are not satisfied that you act justly.

Fore. How?

Scan. You are not satisfied, I say. — I am loath to discourage you — but it is palpable that you are not satisfied.

Fore. How does it appear, Mr. Scandal? I think I am very well satisfied.

Scan. Either you suffer yourself to deceive yourself ; or you do not know yourself.

Fore. Pray explain yourself.

Scan. Do you sleep well o' nights?

Fore. Very well.

Scan. Are you certain? you do not look so.

Fore. I am in health, I think.

Scan. So was Valentine this morning; and looked just so.

Fore. How! am I altered any way? I don't perceive it.

Scan. That may be, but your beard is longer than it was two hours ago.

Fore. Indeed! bless me! [1]

[DU BOIS, ALCESTE.]

Alc.   Ah! que d'amusement!

[1] *Love for Love*, iii. 4 (p. 255 f.).

Veux-tu parler?
Du B. Monsieur, il faut faire retraite.
Alc. Comment?
Du B. Il faut d'ici déloger sans trompette.
Alc. Et pourquoi?
Du B. Je vous dis qu'il faut quitter ce lieu.
Alc. La cause?
Du B. Il faut partir, Monsieur, sans dire adiou.
Alc. Mais par quelle raison me tiens-tu ce langage?
Du B. Par la raison, Monsieur, qu'il faut plier bagage.
Alc. Ah! je te casserai la tête assurément,
  Si tu ne veux, maraud, t'expliquer autrement.[1]

More conscious imitation of the device
appears in Crowne, who studied the Frenchman's dialogue more carefully than any other
dramatist of the period. Even in plays containing no adapted scenes or borrowed characters he frequently imitated the repetition
of Molière. *City Politics* furnishes a typical
illustration, as a comparison with a well-
known scene in *L'Avare* will show.

[PIETRO *is talking with the* PODESTA.]

Piet. . . . Great honours, to my knowledge, are
design'd you: no less than the high office of Lord
Treasurer.
Pod. Lord Treasurer?

[1] *Le Misanthrope*, iv. 4.

Piet. Sir, I speak what I know; 'twill be some time before you come to it; and the Viceroy will expect you to sacrifice to him the doctor, bricklayer, Florio —

Pod. Ay, and my father, too, if he were alive; and shou'd hang 'em all. Lord Treasurer!

Piet. I hope, my lord, you won't refuse some oaths — and —

Pod. Nothing! I'll refuse nothing, sir, for such honour as this. Lord Treasurer!

Piet. I'll acquaint his highness with your arrival. You must be willing to suffer some attendance, the common affliction of all courtiers.

Pod. I'll do or suffer anything for so much glory as this Lord Treasurer!

Piet. Your most humble servant, my lord!

[*Exit* PIET.

Pod. Your most humble servant, sir. Lord Treasurer! to what grandeur am I rising?[1]

[HARPAGON, VALÉRE.]

Harp. . . . Il s'engage à la prendre sans dot.

Val. Sans dot?

Harp. Oui.

Val. Ah! je ne dis plus rien. Voyez-vous? voilà une raison tout à fait convaincante; il se faut rendre à cela.

Harp. C'est pour moi une épargne considérable.

Val. Assurément, cela ne reçoit point de contradiction. Il est vrai que votre fille vous peut représenter

[1] *City Politics*, v. (p. 196 f.).

que le mariage est une plus grande affaire qu'on ne put
croire ; . . .

Harp. Sans dot.

Val. Vous avez raison : voilà qui décide tout, cela
s'entend. Il y a des gens qui pourroient vous dire
qu'en de telles occasions l'inclination d'une fille est une
chose sans doute où l'on doit avoir de l'égard ; . . .

Harp. Sans dot.

Val. Ah ! il n'y a pas de réplique à cela : on le sait
bien ; qui diantre peut aller là contre ? Ce n'est pas
qu'il n'y ait quantité de pères qui aimeroient mieux
ménager la satisfaction de leur filles que l'argent qu'ils
pourroient donner ; . . .

Harp. Sans dot.

Val. Il est vrai : cela ferme la bouche à tout, *sans
dot.* Le moyen de résister à une raison comme celle-
là ? [1]

Another device in Molière's dialogue was
the employment of dramatic irony in *qui-
pro-quo* situations. Of course nothing is
more frequent in Spanish comedies of intrigue
than equivoke. Half the situations are the
result of mistakes and misunderstandings.
Indeed, it was from the Spanish and the Italian
that Molière borrowed the device. But his
treatment of it can easily be distinguished
from that typical of the comedy of intrigue.

[1] *L'Avare*, i. 5.

In the latter all the humor comes from the situations — any other set of persons with the same relations would provide just as laughable a scene. In Molière the peculiar traits of the characters taking part in the situation furnish half the comedy. Every one familiar with his masterpieces will recognize this to be true, but traces of such treatment appear even in so early a play as *Le Dépit Amoureux*. An examination of the *qui-pro-quo* scenes in *The Gentleman Dancing Master* will show that Wycherley in altering the dialogue of the Spanish play he was adapting took hints from Molière. The comic effectiveness of the following scene, for instance, depends to a very considerable extent on the character of Don Diego.

[GERRARD, *the lover, has been passed off on* DON DIEGO, *who prides himself on never being deceived, as a dancing master sent by* PARIS, *who expects to marry* HIPPOLITA *on the morrow.*]

Re-enter DON DIEGO.

Don. Come, have you done?
Hip. O, my father again!
Don. Come, now let us see you dance.
Hip. Indeed I am not perfect yet: pray excuse me

till the next time my master comes.   But when must
he come again, father?

Don. Let me see — friend, you must needs come
after dinner again, and then at night again, and so
three times to-morrow too.   If she be not married to-
morrow, (which I am to consider of,) she will dance a
corant in twice or thrice teaching more; will she not? for
'tis but a twelve-month since she came from Hackney-
school.

Ger. We will lose no time, I warrant you, sir, if she
be to be married to-morrow.

Don. True, I think she may be married to-morrow;
therefore, I would not have you lose any time, look you.

Ger. You need not caution me, I warrant you, sir. —
Sweet scholar, your humble servant : I will not fail you
immediately after dinner.

Don. No, no, pray do not; and I will not fail to
satisfy you very well, look you.

Hip. He does not doubt his reward, father, for his
pains.   If you should not, I would make that good to him.[1]

Such conscious or unconscious reproduction
of the devices of staccato effect, repetition,
and dramatic irony was sporadic.   The only
dramatist whose dialogue was appreciably
colored by imitation of Molière was Crowne,
and even in his case the coloring was faint.
The explanation is that the dramatists who

[1] *The Gentleman Dancing Master*, ii. 2 (p. 170 f.).

had any decided notions about dialogue held
to an ideal directly opposed to Molière's
practice, and accordingly no more attempted
to reproduce his style than they did his plot-
structure. It should not be inferred, however, that the brilliant wit of Restoration
comedy was the result of English literary tradition. In fact, the influence of models
was notable only in the case of John Dryden,
and his models were not the pre-Restoration
dramatists, but the metaphysical poets. He
was in particular influenced by two of the
leaders, — by Donne, who applied all the
subtlety developed by an early scholastic
education to the refinement of far-fetched
metaphors and impossible hyperboles and
labyrinths of paradoxical logic, and by Cowley,
who escaped from the turmoil of religious wars
and the more distracting confusions of chang-
ing beliefs and wavering systems of thought
into a world where he devoted himself to
expressing metaphysical abstractions in all
the novel, ingenious, and subtle images which
his quick fancy and a talent for facile imitation provided. Dryden's *Astrea Redux* contains metaphors as far-fetched as any in

Donne, and his *Annus Mirabilis* vies with Cowley in the abundance of witty conceits. When Dryden forsook panegyrical verse for the more lucrative form of drama, he naturally retained some of this conception of style. This fact explains his definition of wit in comedy as sharpness of conceit [1] and his belief that the chief ornament of dialogue was repartee,[2] a constant fusillade of similitudes, paradoxes, antitheses, phrased with the utmost point to produce a brilliant impression. Examples of the device occur in his first play,[3] but the liveliest dialogue in his comic writing is to be found in the tilts between Wildblood and Jacintha in *An Evening's Love*. A short passage will show how the conceit of the metaphysical poets has been transformed into dartling wit.

Jac. I see there's no hope of reconcilement with you; and therefore I give it over as desperate.

Wild. You have gained your point, you have my money; and I was only angry, because I did not know 'twas you who had it.

Jac. This will not serve your turn, sir: what I have got, I have conquered from you.

[1] Dryden, *Works*, iii. 244.   [2] *Ibid.*, p. 245.
[3] *E.g.*, *The Wild Gallant*, ii. 1; iii. 2.

Wild. Indeed you use me like one that's conquered; for you have plundered me of all I had.

Jac. I only disarmed you, for fear you should rebel again; for if you had the sinews of war, I am sure you would be flying out.[1]

It is indeed true that these tilts were in conception slightly influenced by the love quarrels in *Le Dépit Amoureux* and *Le Tartuffe*. It is also true that Dryden borrowed a surprisingly large number of phrases and passages from Molière. Some of these he utilized merely as characterizing speeches, but generally there was some comparison involved which supplied him with one more similitude to be displayed at the first opportunity. In *Sganarelle*, for instance, he ran across this couplet:

Ah! que j'ai de dépit que la loi n'autorise
A changer de mari comme on fait de chemise![2]

In *The Maiden Queen* he accordingly had Celadon say:—

Yet, for my part, I can live with as few mistresses as any man. I desire no superfluities: only for necessary change or so, as I shift my linen.[3]

---

[1] *An Evening's Love*, iii. 1 (p. 315).
[2] *Sganarelle*, sc. 5.
[3] *The Maiden Queen*, i. 2 (p. 428).

The dilution of thought in this case was, I think, intended to make the paradox more readily apprehensible by an English audience. But all this borrowing of suggestions and expansion of similitudes does not indicate an influence from Molière in Dryden's dialogue. In *Amphitryon* his handling of the French betrays the metaphysical striving not only for novel comparisons, but for paradox and antithesis. No one would expect Dryden with his sense of style to change the admirable neatness and finish of the following passage: —

> *Clé[anthis]*. Mérites-tu, pendard, cet insigne bonheur
> De te voir pour épouse une femme
> d'honneur?
> *Mer[cure]*. Mon Dieu ! tu n'es que trop honnête :
> Ce grand honneur ne me vaut rien.
> Ne sois point si femme de bien,
> Et me romps un peu moins la tête.[1]

Yet what he actually did was to introduce more balance and antithesis in an effort to render the paradox more striking : —

> *Brom[ia]*. Thou deservest not to be yoked with a woman of honour, as I am, thou perjured villain.
> *Merc[ury]*. Ay, you are too much a woman of honour,

[1] Molière's *Amphitryon*, i. 4.

to my sorrow; many a poor husband would be glad
to compound for less honour in his wife, and more quiet.
Pr'ythee, be but honest and continent in thy tongue,
and do thy worst with everything else about thee.[1]

It is clear enough that he had independent
notions of dialogue which agreed ill with the
style of Molière.

The forms of wit in Dryden's dialogue were
therefore a modified continuation of the search
for new and striking similitudes and for antithesis and paradox to be observed in Cowley
and Donne, but the prominence he gave to
wit must be ascribed to an entirely different
cause, to the ideals of the coterie which controlled the society of the day, — that is, as
I said in the beginning of the chapter, to the
taste of the audience before whom he was to
appear. Dryden himself leaves us in no
doubt on this point. He tells us in *An Essay
on the Dramatic Poetry of the Last Age* that
the conversation of his time was much improved over the conversation of Elizabethan
times, that in his time

the fire of the English wit, which was before stifled
under a constrained, melancholy way of breeding, began

[1] Dryden's *Amphitryon*, ii. 2 (p. 50 f.).

first to display its force, by mixing the solidity of our nation with the air and gaiety of our neighbours. This being granted to be true, it would be a wonder if the poets, whose work is imitation, should be the only persons in three kingdoms who should not receive advantage by it; or, if they should not more easily imitate the wit and conversation of the present age than of the past.[1]

What Dryden did not see was that the peculiar quality in the "air and gayety of our neighbors" was intimately related to the European movement of which Cowley and Donne and the whole metaphysical school were merely one manifestation. This is not the place to discuss the complex causes of the movement, which scholars have traced to literary forces and to political, social, and religious conditions.[2] It is sufficient to note that it was dominant in Italy in the first half of the seventeenth century under the name of *secentismo*, reaching its best-known expression in Marino, and that in France of the same period it assumed the form of preciosity. In both countries, as in England, the movement was characterized by a search for unexpected

[1] Dryden, *Works*, iv. 241 f.
[2] Cf. Belloni, p. 456 ff.; Corradino.

antitheses, striking paradoxes, and subtle or surprising comparisons. This search did not prevail only in literature. The man who possessed "wit" was the social idol of the time. Marino was on his return from Paris escorted into his native city of Naples through an arch of triumph, accompanied by the shouting throngs of his fellow-citizens, who at once made him president of their academy. The worship of *bel esprit* among the fashionable circles of Paris is incomparably satirized in *Les Précieuses Ridicules*. One whole scene is taken up with the infatuation for *beaux esprits* and their enigmas, epigrams, and impromptus.

Now it is interesting to observe that the men who were to become the leaders in Restoration social circles traveled extensively in those countries. Buckingham, before he was seventeen, had lived in Florence and Rome in as great state as the native princes,[1] and subsequently passed several years at Paris in the vicinity of the *Palais Royale*.[2] Rochester spent part of his youth in Italy,[3]

[1] Cf. Burghclere, p. 21.   [2] *Ibid.*, pp. 68 f., 71.
[3] Cf. Burnet, p. 5.

and he told Burnet that his studies had been
chiefly in "the Comical and witty Writings
of the Ancients and Moderns," "the Modern
French and Italian as well as the English." [1]
Dorset also traveled in Italy. I have already
shown how familiar with French society
Etheredge and Wycherley had become before
beginning their dramatic career in London.
It was this group of men, acquainted with
the polished society of Italy and France and
the prevalent worship of wit, that is, with
the foreign "air and gayety," to use Dryden's phrase, who became the idols of the
English courtly society and thus modified
"the solidity of our nation." Rochester
was admired because "he had a strange Vivacity of thought, and vigour of expression :
his Wit had a subtility and sublimity both,
that were scarce imitable. When he used
Figures they were very lively, and yet far
enough out of the Common Road." [2] He was
so extravagantly pleasant when inflamed
with wine that many, to be the more diverted
by his humor, engaged him deeper in intem-

[1] Burnet, pp. 28, 27, 7.
[2] *Ibid.*, p. 7.

perance.[1] Buckingham, it is said, was mightily praised for the wit he displayed one afternoon in a theater. An actress in one of Dryden's plays spoke the line,

> My wound is great, because it is so small,

and then paused as if in distress. The Duke rose at once from his seat in a box and "added, in a loud ridiculing voice:

> Then 'twould be greater were it none at all!" [2]

The audience was not shocked by this insolent behavior. On the contrary, its delight in wit was so great that it "hissed the poor woman off the stage ; and would never bear her appearance in the rest of her part." [3]

It is the worship of wit, demonstrated in this and other ways, that explains the dialogue of Restoration comedy. Etheredge, endowed with a very considerable literary talent, produced in his comedies merely a polished imitation of the most sparkling dialogue in the circle of courtly wits with whom he mingled intimately after his first play. Yet this transcript from life simply reveals *secentismo* and preciosity modified and clarified

[1] Cf. Burnet, p. 12.   [2] Spence, p. 47.   [3] *Loc. cit.*

by the "solidity," that is, the native common
sense, of the English. How far this simplification had gone under the chastening influence of English conditions may be seen in
the handling of similitudes : —

Court[al]. That which troubles me most is, we lost
the hopes of variety, and a single intrigue in love is as
dull as a single plot in a play, and will tire a lover worse
than t'other does an audience.

Free[man]. We cannot be long without some underplots in this town ; let this be our main design, and if
we are anything fortunate in our contrivance, we shall
make it a pleasant comedy.[1]

The handling of paradox is equally effective:

Gat[ty]. Truly you seem to be men of great employment, that are every moment rattling from the
eating-houses to the playhouses, from the playhouses
to Mulberry Garden ; that live in a perpetual hurry
and have little leisure for such an idle entertainment [as
making love].

Court[al]. Now would not I see thy face for the
world ; if it should be but half so good as thy humour
thou wouldst dangerously tempt me to dote upon thee,
and, forgetting all shame, become constant.[2]

A single reading of another passage will show
how much more gaiety Etheredge put into

[1] *She Would if She Could*, iii. 1 (p. 161).
[2] *Ibid.*, ii. 1 (p. 143).

repartee than Dryden with his literary models
was able to impart.

Enter the Women [ARIANA *and* GATTY], *and after
them* COURTAL *at the lower door, and* FREEMAN *at the
upper on the contrary side.*

Court. By your leave, ladies.

Gat. I perceive you can make bold enough without
it.

Free. Your servant, ladies.

Aria. Or any other ladies that will give themselves
the trouble to entertain you.

Free. 'Slife, their tongues are as nimble as their heels.

Court. Can you have so little good-nature to dash
a couple of bashful young men out of countenance, who
came out of pure love to tender you their service?

Gat. 'Twere pity to baulk 'em, sister.

Aria. Indeed, methinks they look as if they never
had been slipped before.

Free. Yes, faith, we have had many a fair course in
this paddock, have been very well fleshed, and dare
boldly fasten. [*They kiss their hands with a little force.*

Aria. Well, I am not the first unfortunate woman
that has been forced to give her hand where she never
intends to bestow her heart.[1]

In view of the profound influence of Molière
on Etheredge, it may be well to remember
that in this feature of his dialogue the English

---

[1] *She Would if She Could*, ii. 1 (p. 141 f.).

playwright was in complete opposition to his French master. There was nothing Molière found more ridiculous than the striving for wit among the *précieux*. Every one recalls the ninth scene of *Les Précieuses Ridicules* as evidence on this point, but a more sarcastic attack is the untranslatable speech of Élise in *La Critique de l'École des Femmes*.

La jolie de façon de plaisanter pour des courtisans! et qu'un homme montre d'esprit lorsqu'il vient vous dire : 'Madame, vous êtes dans la place Royale, et tout le monde vous voit de trois lieues de Paris, car chacun vous voit de bon oeil,' à cause que Boneuil est un village à trois lieues d'ici ! Cela n'est-il pas bien galant et bien spirituel? Et ceux qui trouvent ces belles rencontres, n'ont-ils pas lieu de s'en glorifier? [1]

This passage illustrates the spirit of Molière's style. The effectiveness of his dialogue, with all its incomparable gaiety and unflagging verve, is dependent on character and not on sharpness of conceit. Dorine in *Le Tartuffe* is witty enough, but she is so, not from the use of any figures of speech, but from the characteristic impertinence and common sense she everywhere displays. It was this quality

[1] *La Critique de l'École des Femmes*, sc. 1.

in Molière's style that was influential in calling forth the grace and ease and liveliness of
Etheredge's literary gift. Nevertheless, despite its vivacity, his dialogue is not that of
Molière, which with all its gaiety and high
spirits yet contrives to make us feel the ridiculous side of our follies and foibles. Etheredge, on the contrary, reproduces the life
and talk of the idle, intriguing, heartless young
men of his day, not for the purpose of satire,
but with an air of careless indifference, with
never a glance at serious matters, with entire
absorption in the panorama before him. Yet
it was this very faithfulness that made his
dialogue more influential than Dryden's, for,
in Restoration comedy, he was the first
writer with brilliance enough to succeed conspicuously in transferring to the stage that
striving after wit which was developing in
the high society of the realm.

In the matter of dialogue Wycherley's
comedies were also more influential than
Dryden's. Coming out in quick succession,
they drew all eyes to the yet novel style of
writing and made familiar to every playgoer
the vivid, witty, satirical transcripts from

contemporary life. His dialogue of course furnishes abundant proof of his study of Molière. Besides the employment of devices mentioned earlier in the chapter, there are many adapted passages in which he retained much of the Frenchman's manner, even where the variations from the original were most considerable. How true this is may be seen by comparing the first half of the second act of *The Plain Dealer*, which is as good dialogue as he ever wrote, with the corresponding scene in *Le Misanthrope*.[1] It is nevertheless true that he reproduced in his dialogue even less of the spirit of Molière's than Etheredge had, for he displayed in even greater profusion various forms of metaphysical wit chastened by the influence of daily conversation. His pages sparkle with the kind of brilliancy most admired in the gay society of the time. His first play flashes with similitudes like this :—

Val[entine]. You are as unmerciful as the physician who with new arts keeps his miserable patient alive and in hopes, when he knows the disease is incurable.
Vin[cent]. And you, like the melancholy patient,

[1] *Op. cit.*, iii. 4.

mistrust and hate your physician, because he will not comply with your despair.[1]

His paradoxes are more numerous than Etheredge's. The close of *Love in a Wood* reveals his fondness for this kind of cynicism :—

Lyd[ia]. But if I could be desperate now and give you up my liberty, could you find in your heart to quit all other engagements, and voluntarily turn yourself over to one woman, and she a wife too? could you away with the insupportable bondage of matrimony?

Ran[ger]. You talk of matrimony as irreverently as my Lady Flippant: the bondage of matrimony! no —

The end of marriage now is liberty.

And two are bound — to set each other free.[2]

These devices are used in profusion in passages of repartee. He began early : —

Gripe. Where is your parson?

Dap[perwit]. What! you would not revenge yourself upon the parson?

Gripe. No, I would have the parson revenge me upon you ; he should marry me.[3]

It is very easy to understand why the circle that kept Rochester drunk and applauded

---

[1] *Love in a Wood*, v. 5 (p. 111).

[2] *Ibid.*, v. 6 (p. 123).

[3] *Ibid.* (p. 122).

the insolence of Buckingham should be
dazzled by such scintillation and should with
open arms receive the young author into its
most exclusive revels and merrymakings. It
is this association with utterly heartless and
profligate courtiers that helps to explain his
even greater departure from Molière in his
last two plays, with their uncompromising
realism and their unrelenting, coarse, violent,
at times even fierce, satire. No one hears
even after the most brilliant coruscation the
peals of laughter that ring in many a scene
of Molière.

The climax and perfection of Restoration
dialogue is to be found in the comedy of
William Congreve. I can think of nothing
more adequate than the praise of Hazlitt.
"It is the highest model of comic dialogue.
Every sentence is replete with sense and
satire, conveyed in the most polished and
pointed terms. Every page presents a shower
of brilliant conceits, is a tissue of epigrams
in prose, is a new triumph of wit, a new conquest over dullness. The fire of artful raillery
is nowhere else so well kept up." [1]   Yet this

[1] Hazlitt, *Works*, viii. **71.**

is not the result merely of a supreme literary gift. It is simply further evidence of the chastened forms of *secentismo* and preciosity lingering in English high society at the end of the century. Indeed, Congreve declared the banquet-hall of Ralph, Earl of Montague, still echoed with the similitudes and paradoxes abounding in his comedy,[1] and his declaration is corroborated by the plays themselves. For, to quote Hazlitt again, his dialogue "bears every mark of being what he himself in the dedication of one of his plays tells us that it was, a spirited copy taken off and carefully revised from the most select society of his time, exhibiting all the sprightliness, ease, and animation of familiar conversation, with the correctness and delicacy of the most finished composition."[2]

The result is not an individual creation, — it is merely a culmination. The devices which Etheredge began to copy from the conversation of the coffee-house and the salon, and which Wycherley established behind the footlights, Congreve employed in his bright

---

[1] Cf. dedication to *The Way of the World.*
[2] Hazlitt, *Works*, viii. 71.

and sparkling dialogue.   Naturally, with his fine taste, he made less use of similitudes and handled them with greater skill.   The following piece of repartee is realistic enough to be put into any sailor's mouth: —

Ben. . . . What d'ye mean, after all your fair spooohoo and stroking my cheeks, and kissing, and hugging, what, would you sheer off so? would you, and leave me aground?

Mrs. Frail. No, I'll leave you adrift, and go which way you will.

Ben. What, are you false-hearted, then?

Mrs. Frail. Only the wind's changed.[1]

Equally appropriate is this comparison on the lips of Valentine feigning madness: —

You're a woman, — one to whom Heaven gave beauty, when it grafted roses on a briar.   You are the reflection of Heaven in a pond, and he that leaps at you is sunk.   You are all white, a sheet of lovely, spotless paper, when you first are born; but you are to be scrawled and blotted by every goose's quill.[2]

The remainder of the passage illustrates Congreve's favorite form of wit, paradox: —

Val[entine]. . . . I know you; for I loved a woman, and loved her so long, that I found out a strange thing; I found out what a woman was good for.

[1] *Love for Love,* iv. 3 (p. 276).
[2] *Ibid.* (p. 282).

Tat[*tle*]. Ay, prithee, what's that?

Val. Why, to keep a secret.

Tat. O Lord!

Val. O, exceeding good to keep a secret : for though she should tell, yet she is not to be believed.[1]

He combines it frequently with repartee : —

TATTLE, VALENTINE, SCANDAL, *and* ANGELICA.

Ang. You can't accuse me of inconstancy ; I never told you that I loved you.

Val. But I can accuse you of uncertainty, for not telling me whether you did or not.

Ang. You mistake indifference for uncertainty ; I never had concern enough to ask myself the question.

Scan. Nor good-nature enough to answer him that did ask you ; I'll say that for you, madam.

Ang. What, are you setting up for good-nature?

Scan. Only for the affectation of it, as the women do for ill-nature.

Ang. Persuade your friend that it is all affectation.

Scan. I shall receive no benefit from the opinion ; for I know no effectual difference between continued affectation and reality.

Tat. [*Coming up*]. Scandal, are you in private discourse? anything of secrecy?   [*Aside to* SCANDAL.

Scan. Yes, I dare trust you! we were talking of Angelica's love for Valentine ; you won't speak of it?

Tat. No, no, not a syllable ; — I know that's a secret, for it's whispered everywhere.[2]

[1] *Love for Love*, iv. 3 (p. 282).   [2] *Ibid.*, iii. 3 (p. 240 f.).

Of course all Congreve's dialogue was heightened and polished by a rare genius for expression. No actual conversation ever glistened and glittered with the scintillation that appears, for example, in the second act of *The Way of the World* after Millamant enters. Yet even in such scenes one must admit that no one else has ever combined so much naturalness with so much brilliancy.

After what has been said I hardly need repeat that, neither in Congreve's case nor in Restoration comedy as a whole, was the tone and spirit of the dialogue due to the influence of Molière. On the contrary, despite numerous imitated passages and several borrowed devices, its tone and spirit were really a continuation of the preciosity against which the author of *Les Femmes Savantes* launched some of his most delightful satire. The continuation was not through literary channels, except to a slight degree in the case of John Dryden. The other leading dramatists were merely dipping from the clarified English rivulet of that broad and turbulent current of *secentismo* that flowed through the western countries of seventeenth-century Europe.

This is evident not only from the statements of Dryden and Congreve, but from the occasional complaint of a minor dramatist that

> in this Age Design no Praise can get :
> You cry it Conversation wants and Wit.[1]

It is evident also from the comic types that appear and reappear in successive plays. The universally ridiculous figure is the man who tries to be a wit and can't. He appears variously as the Sparkish or Monsieur Paris of Wycherley, as the country wit of Crowne, as the Petulant, or Witwoud, or Tattle of Congreve. The artificial air of Restoration comedy is therefore due to the artificial standards of the age. Just as the quick but coarse Roman listened with delight to the constant punning of Plautus, or the volatile and unreflecting Italian clapped his hands at the *lazzi*, the gymnastic feats and improvised wit, of his favorite actors, or the romantic but subtle Spaniard found unalloyed pleasure in passion that expressed itself in acrostics, in pathos that poured forth a flood of conceits, in sorrow that had leisure to marshal a whole

[1] Cf. prologue to Durfey's *Fond Husband*.

battery of *agudezas*, so the courtly rakes of the Restoration found in the dialogue of the leading dramatists the most brilliant employment of the wit which it was their chief ambition to display in conversation.

CHAPTER VIII

THE CLOSE OF THE PERIOD

THE comedy of manners developed by Molière was, as we have seen, established in England in the decade between 1664 and 1674, but the previous chapters have made it clear that the type was wondrously transformed by the very men who did most to create its vogue in London. Coincident with this development of a new variety, the minor dramatists in the decade of the seventies borrowed from Molière right and left in the concoction of their jumbled intrigues. The influence of the reigning style appeared, however, in the dim reflection of manners in all these busy plots. The scene was frequently Mulberry Garden or the coffee-house or the tavern or a boudoir or a drawing-room, and the amorous intrigue was supposed to correspond more or less closely with the diversions of the killing sparks of the day. Such writers as Mrs. Behn and Thomas Durfey carried this contaminated intrigue comedy through the eighties, and indeed it was the common form to the close of the period. The purer variety of comedy of manners was perpetuated by John Crowne. This diffident writer supplemented his lack of originality by adapting plots and characters from Molière and by frequent imitation of his manner of conducting dialogue. But Crowne was too conscientious a workman not to adjust all his borrowings to his independent purposes. He was too conscientious, also, to pander to the tastes of his audience by impudent intrigue or indecent wit. He could not escape the overwhelming influence of Restoration social life and ideals, as one sees all too clearly in the plot of *The Country Wit* or the character of Camilla in *The Married Beau*, but the moral tone of his comedies is not so perverted as the spirit of the age would lead one to expect. From the fact that he gave to his style a literary finish that reminds one at times of Congreve yet did not care much to spin bright webs of repartee, we may also infer that he did not share the prevalent admiration for the incessant crackling of similitude and paradox.

As successful as Crowne, but less consonant with the standard set by Etheredge and Wycherley, was Thomas Shadwell. He professed himself a follower of Ben Jonson, and he did catch exactly the point of view of the Jacobean master. Even after the amorous intrigues of *Epsom Wells* he declared

> he'd have it understood,
> By representing few ill Wives, he wou'd
> Advance the Value of the many Good.[1]

The animus of his whole work shows that this defense was not so entirely casuistical as would appear on the surface. The unescapable influence of contemporary comedy of manners made itself felt also in the faithfulness with which he reproduced the slang and cant and passing antipathies of London life. For the study of that period his *Squire of Alsatia* is an invaluable document. As a piece of literature it is well-nigh worthless, for it not only possesses none of the wit of Etheredge or Congreve, but it has none of the finish of Dryden or Crowne.

In a theater peopled by such mediocrities appeared, at the beginning of the nineties,

[1] Shadwell, *Works*, ii. 288.

that astonishing youth, William Congreve, destined to carry the English imitation of Molière's comedy of manners to its highest point. On his arrival from the country he had with him a play, *The Old Bachelor*, which revealed his acquaintance with Molière but which was constructed as a comedy of intrigue with five threads of action. Inspired by the success of this first play and by the desire to excel in the art which had brought him the warm friendship of the literary dictator of the age, the young author devoted himself to a more serious study of the great Frenchman who had started Wycherley and Etheredge on their successful careers.

The effect was obvious at once, as a brief review of his plays will show. In *The Double Dealer*, as he avowed in the epistle dedicatory, his effort was to imitate the French. A consideration of the similarities between it and *Le Tartuffe* will reveal how well he had learned Molière's method. Each play is taken up with presenting a hypocrite and the evil effects of his hypocrisy on the life of the family that has befriended him ; in Molière the chief interest is in the characters; in Congreve this

interest is not very successfully satisfied, for
the best work in the play is satire on society.
Each playwright endeavors to hold the attention until the very end by allowing the
hypocrite to succeed in every scheme until
he brings ruin on himself by excess of confidence. Each devotes nearly all of the
first two acts to exposition, and consequently
fails to secure liveliness of movement. In
the rest of the play Molière brings in more
incident than Congreve, although the latter
has more intrigue in the last act than in all
the preceding put together. Each alternates
serious scenes with genuine comedy. In the
third act of *The Double Dealer*, after Lady
Touchwood's arousing her husband's suspicion of Mellefont and her conferring with
Maskwell, Congreve brings in some comic
scenes ending with the matchless Froth-Brisk
dialogue. So in the fifth act of *Le Tartuffe*
Madame Pernelle is brought in to relieve the
somber tone with the richest comic effects.
There is, too, throughout *The Double Dealer*
a very good motivation, in which, however,
Congreve falls below Molière. These similarities of method are the more striking be-

cause the incidents in the two plays are almost
entirely different. Congreve was an independent artist, but he profited by a study of
Molière's practice.

Look now at *Love for Love*, which owes even
less to Molière. Sir Sampson Legend is the
heartless father who drives his son into a re-
bellious attitude and who becomes the rival
of his son only to lose in the end, just as Harpagon does in *L'Avare*. The movement in
the first two acts, which, as in *L'Avare*, are
largely taken up with exposition, is slower
than in the French masterpiece. Though Congreve made no exceptional effort to observe
the unities, the effect of contemporary example and of Molière's practice is apparent.
The scene alternates between Valentine's
lodgings and a room in Foresight's house,
and the time is part of two days. Unity of
action is not preserved perfectly, since the
Foresight-Scandal episode has almost no
connection with the main plot. But this
underplot serves the purpose of the whole
play — which is to satirize the society of the
day, just as the aim of *L'Avare* is to turn a
single vice into ridicule. The motivation is

not perfect ; it is not clear what Valentine
hopes to accomplish by his simulation of
madness, nor is the Frail-Tattle affair sufficiently prepared for ; but in the motivation
as a whole the play is not far behind *L'Avare*.
It is equal to that piece in sustaining the interest to the very end, and it is even more
successful in the way that end is brought
about, — not by a *deus ex machina*, but from
within the play itself. In this production
Congreve accordingly displays again distinctive features of the French master's craft.

In *The Way of the World*, in which there is
very little borrowing from Molière, the effect
of the French technique is equally apparent.
Observe that this comedy has the same
purpose as *Le Misanthrope :* Molière wishes
to depict the *beau monde* of Paris ; Congreve
wishes to present the high life of London.
The Frenchman is, as usual, more interested
in the portrayal of character, the Englishman
in the satire on society. Observe, too, that
there is the same want of incident. The first
two acts in both plays are again largely
devoted to exposition. The fourth act of
Congreve's is slow, but the third and fifth

have more movement than the last three of *Le Misanthrope*. Most of the action, too, passes in Lady Wishfort's house. Observe, lastly, the same device for sustaining the suspense. In the first act of each play no woman appears. The listener is kept in uncertainty about the *dénouement* until the very close of each play. Here Congreve falls behind Molière. Mirabell's plot against Lady Wishfort to secure her niece Millamant is not perfectly plausible, and Fainall's counterplot to secure a fortune from Lady Wishfort is not perfectly clear. Here we miss the lucid and convincing motivation of *Le Misanthrope*. The last act, too, is not the inevitable consequence of the preceding action, as it is in the French masterpiece. It is so complicated that it is confusing, and the *dénouement* is brought about by the *deus ex machina* of the suddenly discovered deed of conveyance of Mrs. Fainall's property to Mirabell. In spite of these shortcomings the general features of the plot-management are here, as in the two preceding comedies, the same as in Molière.

This survey reveals, then, a considerable

influence from the great French genius upon
the general dramatic method of Congreve.
In all his comedies but the first he manages
the course of the action in the same way as
Molière — he employs a long exposition taking
up most of two acts, he seldom changes the
scene, and he holds the interest till the close
by deferring much of the incident till the final
act. He shows a care in motivation which,
though faulty in places, approaches the care
of the Frenchman in his best pieces, a care
which was unknown in the comedies of the
Elizabethan and Jacobean periods of the elder
drama and which was extremely rare in Restoration comedy. What is equally significant, he gave an earnestness to the main
thread in each plot that inevitably reminds
one of the serious element in the French
masterpieces. Indeed, the action of *The
Double Dealer* is essentially tragic, and an
atmosphere of gravity hangs about the
central intrigues of *The Way of the World*
also. Even *Love for Love* receives a seriousness of treatment, contains a recognition of
the fact that life may have some meaning,
very rare in previous comedy of the period.

What is more significant, after his first effort he constructed plots of the same kind as those in Molière's masterpieces — plots in which the action is invented to serve the purpose of the play, — that is, to satirize the foibles and vices of society. He did not adopt Molière's practice completely, for he in no case made all parts of the intrigue illustrate a controlling thesis; he felt it necessary to introduce underplots, which frequently satirize a different foible, apparently on the model of the Fidget episode in *The Country Wife*. But in the conduct of retributive justice in his main plot the Frenchman was the major influence.

If we look for special cases of imitation that will fully establish our belief that Congreve owes the above features of his method to a study of Molière, they are easily found. Some devices of exposition have already been mentioned: in *The Double Dealer* and *The Way of the World* the hero and his confidant open the action as they do in *Le Misanthrope;* in *Love for Love* the hero and his servant, as in *Le Dépit Amoureux* and several of the lighter pieces of Molière; in *The Old Bachelor* and *The Way of the World* the entrance of the women is deferred till the second act on the model of *Le Misanthrope*. Other features of Congreve's dramatic method strengthen the conclusion. Examine the close of the second act of *The Old Bachelor* or of the fourth of *The Double Dealer* or *Love for Love*, and then think of the increased briskness of action at the end of the third act of *L'Avare* or *Le Tartuffe*, and it becomes clear that Congreve adopted Molière's characteristic method of closing an act. The soliloquies of his second or of his last piece, when compared with those of *L'École des Maris* or *L'École des Femmes*, reveal another phase of the influence. His familiarity with the great Frenchman affected his technique in an even more intimate manner, — it conditioned the working of his imagination. The coffee-house that furnished most of the background for the first act of *The Way of the World*, the lodgings of a young gentleman in the first act of *Love for Love*, — these realistic, commonplace interiors reveal how constantly such places as the room in Orgon's home or the salon in Célimène's hovered before the mind of the young Englishman. Certain it is from the foregoing examination that, though Congreve could provide all the material for his plays by his own keen observation of the life in which he moved, he studied Molière for suggestions, absorbed the Frenchman's manner, and adopted his dramatic method.

In the treatment of character his indebtedness is also evident. Nothing can be clearer than the Mrs. Plyant scenes in *The Double Dealer*.[1] Even the original, Béline, is not so effectively presented. There is nothing sharper or more incisive in *L'Avare* than the scene between Valentine and his father in *Love for Love*.[2] Célimène herself is not so gay and light as Millamant. Most of his characters have so much of this definiteness of presentation and of this dramatic heightening characteristic of Molière's that Hazlitt declared he would rather see them on the stage than any other figures in English comedy.[3] His comic characters resemble Molière's in another feature. They are not drawn with

[1] *Op. cit.*, ii. 1 (p. 125 ff.); iv. 1 (p. 152 f.). Cf. *Les Femmes Savantes*, i. 4.
[2] *Op. cit.*, ii. 1 (p. 226 ff.).
[3] Cf. Hazlitt, *Works*, viii. 74.

the complexity of Shakspere's heroes and heroines. Their comic effectiveness is based on some extravagance which is thrown into sharp opposition with the dictates of good taste or good sense. No one can mistake such basal incongruity in Lady Froth or Lady Plyant or Tattle or Foresight. Even Madame Pernelle does not offer a greater contradiction. Of course Congreve was not always at his best. He was never very successful in good characters, and he was often too profuse with his wit; but his satiric conceptions show very clearly that he had studied with profit Molière's method of character portrayal no less than he had the other features of that genius's dramatic practice.

Naturally, this historical account has emphasized Congreve's indebtedness to Molière. But what impresses one most on first reading his comedies is his aptitude for this kind of writing, his genius for the theater. Even a genius, however, is never absolutely original, is affected by his environment profoundly, — indeed, must learn many lessons from his predecessors. It was therefore inevitable that Congreve should become acquainted with previous Restoration comedy, which we have seen was so largely affected by Molière ; it was certain he would read closely the comedies of William Wycherley, recognized as the best playwright of the period, and it was all but inevitable that he should turn to Wycherley's well-known source. His native genius for the theater and his innate fine taste would at once detect the superiority of the Frenchman's manner and methods, and the admiration thus begotten in the youthful aspirant for stage honors would necessarily incite him to more enthusiastic study. For it must be remembered that Congreve was not much over twenty-one when he produced his first play, and had hardly entered his thirties when he retired from the stage for good. The wonder is, then, not that he adopted so much from Molière, but that he showed such striking originality in these creations of his young manhood. For in following a model he was but repeating the practice of Molière himself, who at the beginning of his career imitated the Italians closely and in all his work was influenced by them, — he was but following the example set by the greatest genius of his own country, for every student of Shakspere is familiar with the powerful influence Marlowe exerted on the youthful productions of his transcendent successor.

It should therefore occasion no surprise to discover that Congreve took very considerable hints from Molière. One should rather inquire whether the influence did not go deeper, whether it did not affect Congreve's point of view in dealing with comic material. It may be answered at once that the points of view of the two writers are much alike. Both are largely impersonal in their treatment of life. Molière's aloofness is tinged with sympathy, which appears in so early a character as Arnolphe of *L'École des Femmes* and is unmistakable in Alceste of *Le Misanthrope*. Congreve is impersonal in a colder way. His attitude toward his creations is one of unobtrusive superiority, a careless indifference coming from a just sense of the perspective of things. But above this cynical attitude of the man of the world with his fine intellect and his fine taste, there appears no higher viewpoint, no broader outlook. He ignores all moral implications of his theme, and is utterly oblivious to the social meaning of his treatment. He knows the narrow field of high society, but he lacks the broad comprehension of all life characteristic of Molière, that insight into the springs of action and the deeps of character conspicuous in *Le Tartuffe* and *Le Misanthrope*. Despite these differences Congreve is nearer Molière in his attitude toward his material than any other English writer of comedy, and the student cannot resist the conclusion that it was under his influence that Congreve developed so quickly what was of course an inherent susceptibility and tendency of his nature.

Congreve was the last man to embody fully the ideals of the courtly circle. Even before he entered the world of high society there had begun in the theater a movement away from the dominance of courtiers and wits. The Revolution of 1688 did more than shatter forever the absolutism of the king in political affairs. The court of William and Mary was an immensely different place from the court of Charles II. The cold and taciturn William with his Dutch favorites and his absorbing

interest in questions of state had no time for
the theater, and his queen, Mary, was of a
purity so genuine that even political lam-
pooners respected her.   There was not only
no room for the gallantry that had distinguished Charles's circle, but scandal and
gossip were unfailingly discountenanced by
both King and Queen.   Moreover, the transference of the royal residence to Hampton
Court and its later establishment at Ken-
sington removed the royal household entirely
from the center of that gay life which the
theater had been reflecting for a score of years.
Of course the old manner of living and the
usual kinds of diversion continued to flourish,
but political questions at home and distant
campaigns soon began to absorb a good deal
of attention from the playhouse.   After the
Revolution Shadwell complained that

> Our unfrequented Theatre must mourn,
> 'Till the Brave Youths Triumphantly return,[1]

and that the soft men of peace

> eagerly elsewhere in Throngs resort,
> Crowding for Places in the well-fill'd Court.[2]

Southerne in 1691 declared,

---

[1] Shadwell, *Works*, iv. 214.   [2] *Ibid.*

heroes are the same,
A twelvemonth running in pursuit of fame,[1]

so that the ladies, and the dramatists, too,
we infer, deeply regretted the "thin town."
The theater had indeed ceased to be the diversion of the leading men, few but fops attend-
ing, and they meeting with anything but
flattery from the dramatists.[2] The women
accordingly made their taste more respected
than it had been, their complaints becoming
more numerous and much more influential
than ever before.   Southerne omitted a scene
in *Sir Anthony Love* (1691) that Lee might
have acted to great advantage, because he
did not care to "run the venture of offending
the women."[3]   Shadwell assured the ladies
in the prologue to *The Scowrers* (1693) that

the Play's so clean,
The nicest shall not tax it for Obscene.[4]

The defiant Vanbrugh felt it necessary to
reply to the attacks on *The Relapse* (1696)
by averring with brazen disregard for the

[1] Southerne, *Works*, i. 158.
[2] Cf. Shadwell, *Works*, iv. 397 f.
[3] Southerne, *Works*, i. 156.
[4] Shadwell, *Works*, iv. 307.

truth that there was not one woman of real reputation in town but would find it innocent.[1] Congreve also had to take account of the ladies,[2] and he even went so far as to declare to the Princesse Anne "that a play may be with industry so disposed (in spite of the licentious practice of the modern theatre) as to become sometimes an innocent, and not unprofitable entertainment." [3] It was therefore perfectly natural that Jeremy Collier's *Short View* should be acclaimed as a triumphant condemnation of the rule of gallants and wits in the theater. The respectable middle class, with its bourgeois virtues and morals, which had lived its quiet life in retirement all those years since the Restoration of Charles II, now boldly invaded the playhouse and demanded that its prejudices be observed.

All such revolutions are slow. Sir John Vanbrugh, with the instinctive dissent of a realist, revolted from the approaching reformation, declaring that life was not chaste

[1] Cf. Vanbrugh, i. 7.
[2] Cf. epistle dedicatory to *The Double Dealer* (1694).
[3] Dedication to *The Mourning Bride* (1697).

and manners were not pure, and that he was
going to picture conditions as they were. It
was thoroughly consistent with this attitude
that in all parts of his work he exhibited
curiously little study of models, but everywhere displayed a full reliance on his native
sense of the humorous and the dramatically
effective. He apparently made up his plot
as he went along, introducing characters as
needed. In *The Relapse* he had Young
Fashion personate his brother, Lord Foppington, in the country at the home of Sir Tunbelly
Clumsy in order to win the daughter and her
fortune, which had already been pledged
to Lord Foppington. When the true lord
unexpectedly arrived at the Clumsy home,
Young Fashion boldly declared his brother
an impostor, and Sir Tunbelly accordingly
drove the intruder's servants away and locked
the lord himself up in a dog-kennel. Of course
at this point Vanbrugh had to display some
ingenuity in extricating the mistreated fop
from so humiliating a situation. He accordingly had Lord Foppington mention Sir
John Friendly, a neighboring squire, as a
friend of his, though the man had not been

spoken of before in the play and was not to appear after identifying the ill-used dandy. This incident fairly illustrates Vanbrugh's method — the developing of separate situations as the possibilities presented themselves, but without reference to a central theme or a general design. It is unnecessary to remark that he did not study Molière, for it is clear that he paid little attention to the structure of anybody's plays.

His independence appears in other features of his work. The method of character-drawing that Wycherley employed in imitation of Molière, if he had noticed it at all, would have seemed a waste of time. "What is the use," he might have exclaimed to a praiser of *The Plain Dealer*, "when just as many funny situations can be developed without such study? Whenever I see anything laughable in life I copy it and exaggerate it until it is laughable on the stage. Little inconsistencies or failures to follow probability will be overlooked." His use of contrast, however, such as the opposition between Lord Foppington and Sir Tunbelly in *The Relapse*, or that between Sir John Brute and his wife in *The Provoked Wife*, was obviously suggested by *The Plain Dealer* and *The Country Wife*. His absorbing interest in reality led him to adopt also Wycherley's manner of lingering over scenes while the intrigue sleeps. His comedies abound in passages such as the one describing Lord Foppington's manner of life,[1] for he had a keen eye for the ridiculous and took pleasure in presenting it, no matter how long the action had to pause. Yet these passages differ from the similar ones in Wycherley, for the satirical interest is not thrust upon the audience. The acts and words of the characters are allowed to speak for themselves.

Though Vanbrugh fought against the reformation of the theater, he did not worship with the inner circle of gallants and wits. He liked to take his plot out into the country, on which occasions he would reproduce dialect almost as faithfully as Shadwell copied the cant of Alsatia. But even his town gallants do not fire off similitudes and paradoxes in that brilliant pyrotechnic fashion common

[1] Cf. *The Relapse*, ii. 1 (p. 43 ff.).

in Wycherley, Dryden, and Congreve. Although Vanbrugh displayed a considerably greater literary gift than Shadwell, his aim was to portray life realistically, without subjecting the conversation to the for him unfamiliar polish it received at the hands of his distinguished predecessors. In other words, he was not of the exclusive set in high society to which the leaders had belonged — he was not of the coterie.

Yet Vanbrugh was essentially an Englishman of the Restoration. He was in fact closer to the comedy of manners as Etheredge introduced it into England than any other writer of the period. The savage satire that Wycherley indulged in does not appear in his comedies. Lord Foppington, Lady Fanciful, and the Headpiece family are presented with considerably less grace, to be sure, but with much the same detachment that Etheredge used in presenting Sir Fopling Flutter. But Vanbrugh's presentation of manners, I hardly need add, is completely lacking in the sympathy with life and the insight into character that distinguished Molière. To use an old figure, his method is the method of the photographer, who reproduces faithfully but reproduces only the outside. Molière's method is the method of the artist, who transforms what he reproduces so as to omit what is accidental and to reveal what is essential. In this respect Congreve is much closer to Molière than is Vanbrugh. Congreve presents his pictures with artistic delicacy of touch. Vanbrugh paints with a realism that is frequently brutal. But it is not surprising that one who knew nothing of Molière's genius did not catch the comic spirit of the French master. The only influence of Molière on Vanbrugh was the indirect influence through previous English comedy.

Vanbrugh is thus seen to carry on the comedy of manners with a partial loss of the tone of the clique. This divergence from tradition was continued by Farquhar. He hardly belongs in a discussion of Molière's influence, since his knowledge of the great Frenchman was slighter even than Vanbrugh's. His eye was apparently caught by a few scenes as he was turning the pages of Molière in idle moments, but he really knew nothing directly of the spirit of the Frenchman's comedies. Nor was he saturated with the spirit of Restoration comedy. Reared far away from the courtly circle and reaching London when the women and citizens were making their prejudices known, he really marks the close of the period.

That the influence of the coterie was lessening is seen in every feature of his work. He does not spend all his time in presenting the manners of the fine gentlemen and ladies of London. He often places his scenes in country towns and depicts provincial customs. His chief personages have in them something natural and wholesome that is lacking in the creations of his predecessors. His sparks are not so utterly heartless as Etheredge's, and his fine ladies less frequently give way to animal instinct. Sir Harry Wildair has a regard for others that cannot be matched in Congreve, and Mrs. Sullen retains her virtue under trials in which any character in Wycherley or Dryden would have lost hers. More than this, Farquhar follows a different method of presenting his material. The manners are not described in lengthy passages while the action and characterization are at a standstill, — a method which we found was traceable to Molière's influence.   He is skilful enough, in spite of his scorn of regular structure, to weave the picture of manners into his plot.   His figures are kept moving most of the time.   He thus advances a step beyond Vanbrugh in leaving the typical comedy of the Restoration.

He advances beyond Vanbrugh also in the omission of similitudes, paradox, and balance. He makes little effort to be witty.   He does not elaborate or polish his style.   This quality is not the result of the realistic tendency observable in Vanbrugh.   It is rather because he had always been an entire stranger to the forms of metaphysical wit.   His style is not highly literary in any sense.   It is merely the natural effervescence of a buoyant and sprightly disposition.   With him the artificial comedy of the Restoration came to a close, to give place to the sentimental comedy of the eighteenth century with its reflection of a less corrupt but more hypocritical society.

CHAPTER IX

CONCLUSION

THE characteristics of Restoration comedy must now be clear. The two main currents may be designated comedy of manners and comedy of intrigue. The first in particular reflected with the inevitable exaggeration of the theater the life of the ruling coterie of the period, the various diversions of the heartless gallants and airy coquettes who were always on the lookout for some new conquest, the frivolities and affectations of the fops and *précieuses* in the park, at the coffee-house, in the boudoir or the drawing-room, the prejudices and prepossessions of the *beau monde*, its amused contempt for country knights, rustic hoydens, strait-laced citizens, and miserly aldermen, its admiration for sparkling wit and sprightly repartee, — almost the one serious preoccupation of that whole artificial society. The comedy of intrigue endeavored to supply the lack of well-drawn types and vivid pictures from life by a confusing intricacy of action and a bewildering variety of persons, and to make up for the deficiency of genuine wit by a superfluity of indelicate allusion.

Such a comedy bore a natural resemblance to the society which gave it birth. That society manifested no profound interest in the momentous issues that hung upon the political struggles of the period. Its only tribute to religion was a persistent effort to escape all the restraints which any form of morality might impose. All its energies were consequently absorbed in leading the dance through a profligate carnival of the senses. It was therefore incapable of the generous romantic interest of Elizabethan England or of the golden age of Spain. It was totally averse to reflecting on the mystery of life or the problems of destiny. It was interested only in itself and in its own superficial amusements. It could find pleasure only in a theater that would represent brightly colored pictures of the external aspect of its own mundane existence. It could produce only a comedy of manners which should

restrict itself to the entertainment of a coterie.

One may therefore ask whether a product
so intimately related to its period was really
influenced by Molière. One may urge that
Restoration comedy, though possessing very
marked differences from Jacobean comedy
of manners, was after all simply the logical
and inevitable evolution of the court comedy
seen developing under Fletcher and Shirley.
It may be admitted at once that the Restoration would have produced a comedy not
much different from the actual product, even
had Molière never lived. Every period where
a society grows up living a life more or less
apart from the body of the people and thus
fostering an interest in itself, must find expression in some variety of comedy of manners if it find expression in the theater at all.
But the fact remains that the peculiar variety
developed during the Restoration owed a
good deal to Molière. The cases of particular
indebtedness discussed in the previous chapters have surely made it clear that with a
few exceptions the plots best suited to reflect
the conditions of the time were either adapted

from Molière or developed under his influence, that the situations most instinct with comic satire derived their effectiveness from the reproduction in some degree of Molière's spirit, and that the types of character that linger in one's memory may be traced more or less directly to the pages of Molière. This counts for something. But more important is the truth which I hope the preceding chapters have made clear that Restoration comedy, taken as a type, owed its inception and found its development in an imitation of the comedy of manners of Molière, in the process battered and twisted and distorted often almost beyond recognition, but after all an evidence of the influence of that genius whom every Frenchman delights to honor. And the reason why this foreign type, not in its technical features, but in its animating spirit, was more influential than Jonson's comedy of humors or Fletcher's court comedy, is that it was more congenial to a society that was less interested in satirical portraiture or romantic exaggeration than it was in its own mundane existence.

APPENDIX

A LIST OF BORROWINGS

THE following list aims to give only the important direct borrowings from Molière. To trace the indirect indebtedness would be impossible within any reasonable limits. For minor borrowings, such as copied phrases, the reader is referred to the special studies, which are noted in the Bibliography whenever they have come to my notice. Even thus restricted, the notes may be misleading, especially in the treatment of character. For instance, it has been impossible to indicate when a borrowing from Molière included a whole scene and when only a passage from the scene cited. But of course these and other explanations and qualifications, necessary for exactness, would be out of the question here. The various features of each play discussed in the preceding chapters may be traced by reference to the index. Unless otherwise specified, the dates are the most probable dates of production.

I hardly need add that the list below is the result of my own research, but I have used previous investigations for guidance or suggestion. The direct or indirect source of all lists of borrowings has been Langbaine (1691), who delighted to expose plagiarism, and whose wide reading in drama enabled him to detect a great many cases of indebtedness. The first list of borrowings appeared in Jacob (1723), i. 292 ff. An extensive list was drawn up in some detail by Laun and published in *Le Moliériste* under the title, *Les Plagiaires de Molière en Angleterre* (août, 1880, p. 143 ff.; novembre, 1880, p. 235 ff.; janvier, 1881, p. 303 ff.; mai, 1881, p. 52 ff.; août, 1881, p. 137 ff.). The same material had appeared in the notices and appendices of his translation of Molière (1875–6). Charlanne (1906), p. 490 ff., made few changes in Laun. Kerby (1907), p. 115 ff., also drew from second-hand sources. As I did not run across Kerby's monograph till November, 1909, I was unable to derive any advantage from his work. (The only copy I know of is in the Columbia University Library.) In a few cases I have found hints in the scattered notices that occur in histories of English drama, in dictionaries of old plays, in biographies and editions of Molière. For the numerous special studies the reader is again referred to the Bibliography, II.

AMOROUS BIGOT, THE, (1690) by Shadwell. The rivalry of father and son is a reminiscence of *L'Avare*. The scenes in which Hernando appears (act iv.) are a reminiscence of the plot of *Les Précieuses Ridicules*. The relation of Elvire to her mother is a reflection of the *motif* of *L'École des Maris* (probably through *The Country Wife*). Act. iv. (p. 271 f.) was suggested by *L'Avare*, iii. 6, 7, and *Les Femmes Savantes*, i. 4.

AMOROUS WIDOW, OR THE WANTON WIFE, THE, (1670) by Betterton. (1) The stratagem of Cuningham against Lady Laycock, chiefly in acts i. and ii., is adapted freely from *Les Précieuses Ridicules*. (2)

The second plot, the Brittle action, is adapted from
George Dandin (act iii. = *George Dandin,* i.; act iv.
= *George Dandin,* ii. ; act v. = *George Dandin,* iii.),
about a third being pretty closely translated, the
remainder more or less freely adapted.

(1) Merryman = Mascarille (*Les Précieuses Ridicules*) ; Cuningham = La Grange. (2) Sir Peter Pride
= M. de Sotenville (*George Dandin*) ; Lady Pride =
Madame de Sotenville; Lovemore = Clitandre; Barnaby Brittle = George Dandin ; Clodpole = Lubin;
Mrs. Brittle = Angélique ; Damaris = Claudine. Pru-
dence is an imitation of Molière's soubrettes.

AMPHITRYON, OR THE TWO SOSIAS, (1690) by Dryden.
(1) The play is an adaptation of *Amphitryon.*
(2) The Mercury-Phædra intrigue was suggested by
Le Mariage Forcé: act v. 1 (p. 95 ff.) is adapted
from *Le Mariage Forcé,* sc. 9.

ASSIGNATION, OR LOVE IN A NUNNERY, THE, (1672) by
Dryden. Act iii. 1 (p. 417 f.) is freely adapted from
L'Étourdi, ii. 11. Act iv. 4 (p. 443 ff.) is freely
adapted from *Le Tartuffe,* ii. 4. Benito is a free
adaptation of Lélie (*L'Étourdi*).

ATHEIST, OR THE SECOND PART OF THE SOLDIER'S
FORTUNE, THE, (1684) by Otway. The conduct of
Porcia is a reminiscence of *L'École des Femmes,* prob-
ably through *The Country Wife.* The recital by
Beaugard's father of his hard luck at dice (act iii., p.
42) is an alteration of *Les Fâcheux,* ii. 2.

BARGAIN BROKEN, A. See *The Canterbury Guests.*

Beaux' Stratagem, The, (1707) by Farquhar. Act iii. 3 (p. 295 ff.) is freely adapted from *Le Tartuffe*, iv. 5, 6.

Bury Fair (1689) by Shadwell. Cf. *ante*, p. 133 ff. Act i. (p. 121 ff.) is freely adapted from *Le Misanthrope*, ii. 4. Act i. (p. 124 f.) was suggested by *Le Bourgeois Gentilhomme*, iii. 4, or possibly by *La Comtesse d'Escarbagnas*, sc. 2. Act v. (p. 197 f.) was suggested by *Le Misanthrope*, v. 2.

Canterbury Guests, or a Bargain Broken, The, (1694) by Ravenscroft. (1) The play reproduces word for word more than half of *The Careless Lovers*. (2) Act i. 3 was suggested by the character of Sganarelle in *Le Mariage Forcé*. Act ii. 5 is adapted from *Le Mariage Forcé*, sc. 2. Act iii. 1 is adapted from *Le Bourgeois Gentilhomme*, iii. 4. Act v. 1 is adapted from *Monsieur de Pourceaugnac*, ii. 4. Act v. 5 is adapted from *Le Mariage Forcé*, sc. 9.

Careless Lovers, The, (1673) by Ravenscroft. (1) The main action is an adaptation of *Monsieur de Pourceaugnac*. Act iv. (pp. 41–5) is adapted from *Monsieur de Pourceaugnac*, ii. 7, 8; act iv. (pp. 38–40) was suggested by *Les Précieuses Ridicules*, sc. 9, 13; act ii. (pp. 10–16) is adapted from *Le Bourgeois Gentilhomme*, iii. 8–10; act ii. (p. 17 f.) was suggested by *Le Bourgeois Gentilhomme*, i. 2; in act v. (p. 56 f.), the disguise was suggested by *Le Médecin malgré lui*. (2) A minor action was suggested by *An Evening's Love*. There are several episodes.

CAUTIOUS COXCOMB, THE. See *Sir Salomon*.

CHEATS OF SCAPIN, THE, (1677) by Otway. The play is a translation for the stage of *Les Fourberies de Scapin*. Acts i., ii., are translated closely. In act iii., scenes 3–5 are omitted; scenes 7–11 are replaced by new scenes.

CITIZEN TURNED GENTLEMAN, THE. See *Mamamouchi*.

COMICAL REVENGE, OR LOVE IN A TUB, THE, (1664) by Etheredge. The subplot was suggested by *Le Dépit Amoureux*. Cf. *ante*, p. 62 ff.

CONSTANT COUPLE, OR A TRIP TO THE JUBILEE, THE, (1699) by Farquhar. Act ii. 5 (p. 165 f.) was suggested by *Le Médecin malgré lui*, i. 5.

COUNTRY WIFE, THE, (1673) by Wycherley. (1) The play is an adaptation of *L'École des Femmes*, modified in acts iv. and v. by *L'École des Maris*. Act i. 1 (p. 261 ff.) is adapted from *L'École des Femmes*, i. 1; act iv. 2 (p. 313 f.) is adapted from *L'École des Femmes*, ii. 5; act iv. 2 (p. 317 f.) and 4 (p. 333 ff.) were suggested by *L'École des Maris*, ii. 3; act v. 1 (p. 336 ff.) was suggested by *L'École des Maris*, iii. 1–3. (2) The Sparkish-Alithea subplot was suggested by the relations of Léonor and Ariste in *L'École des Maris:* act iii. 2 (p. 296 ff.) was suggested by *L'École des Maris*, ii. 9.

Pinchwife = Arnolphe (*L'École des Femmes*); Mrs. Pinchwife = Agnès; Horner = Horace.

COUNTRY WIT, THE, (1675) by Crowne. (1) *Le Sicilien* is adapted for a minor intrigue: act ii. (pp. 48–51)

is a free adaptation of *Le Sicilien*, sc. 3, 4; act iv.
(pp. 88–96) is adapted from *Le Sicilien*, sc. 9–13.
(2) The main plot was suggested by *Le Tartuffe*:
act i. (p. 19 ff.) is freely adapted from *Le Tartuffe*,
ii. 2, with suggestions from *Le Tartuffe*, i. 5.

(1) Lord Drybone = Don Pèdre (*Le Sicilien*); Betty
Frisque = Isidore; Ramble = Adraste; Merry = Hali.
(2) Sir Thomas = Orgon (*Le Tartuffe*); Isabella =
Dorine. Lady Faddle was suggested by the Comtesse
d'Escarbagnas — *e.g.*, cf. act i. (p. 32 f.) and *La Comtesse d'Escarbagnas*, sc. 2, — and by Bélise: act ii. (p.
37 f.) was suggested by *Les Femmes Savantes*, i. 4.

CUCKOLD IN CONCEIT, THE, (1707) by Vanbrugh. A
translation for the stage of *Sganarelle*, which was never
published.

CURIOUS IMPERTINENT, THE. See *The Married Beau*.

DAMOISELLES À LA MODE, THE, (1667) by Flecknoe.
"This Comedy is taken out of several Excellent
Pieces of Molière. The main plot of the Damoiselles
out of his Precieuses Ridicules; the Counterplot of
Sganarelle, out of his Escole des Femmes, and out of
the Escole des Marys, the two Naturals." This
passage from the preface is given in Lohr, p. 88.
The play has not been accessible to me.

DOUBLE DEALER, THE, (1694) by Congreve. (1) The
plot was suggested by *Le Tartuffe*. Cf. *ante*, p. 195 ff.
Act v. 1 is freely adapted from *Le Tartuffe*, iii. 7.
(2) Act ii. 1 (p. 126 ff.) is adapted from *Les Femmes
Savantes*, i. 4; act iii. 3 (the heroic poem) was sug-

gested by *Les Femmes Savantes*, iii. 2 (the epigram), with free adaptation from *Le Misanthrope*, ii. 4.

Maskwell = Tartuffe ;   Careless = Cléante ;   Lord Touchwood = Orgon ;   Lady Froth = Philaminte (*Les Femmes Savantes*) as a learned lady ;   Sir Paul and Lady Plyant = Chrysale and Philaminte as man and wife.   The conception of Lady Plyant also owes a good deal to Bélise.

DOUBLE DISCOVERY, THE.   See *The Spanish Friar*.

DUMB LADY, OR THE FARRIER MADE PHYSICIAN, THE, (1669) by Lacy.   Cf. *ante*, p. 88 ff.   Act i. is closely adapted from *Le Médecin malgré lui*, i. ;   act ii. is closely adapted from *Le Médecin malgré lui*, ii. ;   act iii. is closely adapted from *Le Médecin malgré lui*, iii. 1–6 ;   act iii. (p. 54 ff.) was suggested by *Les Fourberies de Scapin*, ii. 5 ;   act iv. is freely adapted from *L'Amour Médecin*, i. 4, 3, 6 ;   act v. is very freely adapted from *L'Amour Médecin*, ii. 2–7, with suggestions from *Le Médecin malgré lui*, iii. 11, 9.

ENGLISH FRIAR, OR THE TOWN SPARKS, THE, (1690) by Crowne.   The play is a free adaptation of *Le Tartuffe*.   Act v. (p. 112 ff.) is adapted from *Le Tartuffe*, iv. 3, 5.

Father Finical = Tartuffe ;   Lady Credulous = Orgon ;   Sir Thomas = Elmire (in part) ;   Pansy = Elmire (in part).   Lord Stately is a reminiscence of *La Comtesse d'Escarbagnas*.   *E.g.*, act i. (pp. 32, 35) was suggested by *La Comtesse d'Escarbagnas*, sc. 2.   Lady Pinchgut is an adaptation of Harpagon in *L'Avare*.   Cf. *ante*, p. 158 f.

EPSOM WELLS (1672) by Shadwell. Act iv. (p. 261 ff.) is adapted from *Le Médecin malgré lui*, i. 1–3. Cuff, Kick, and Clodpate are reminiscences of Acaste, Clitandre, and Alceste in *Le Misanthrope*.

EVENING'S LOVE, OR THE MOCK ASTROLOGER, AN, (1668) by Dryden. Act i. 1 (p. 261 f.) is freely adapted from *L'École des Maris*, i. 3. Act iii. 1 (p. 304 ff.) is adapted from *Le Dépit Amoureux*, ii. 6. Act iv. 2 (p. 334 f.) is adapted from *Le Dépit Amoureux*, i. 2. Act iv. 4 (p. 341 ff.) is freely adapted by combination of *Le Dépit Amoureux*, iv. 3 and 4.

Aurelia is adapted from Cathos and Madelon in *Les Précieuses Ridicules:* act iii. 1 (p. 296 f.) was suggested by *Les Précieuses Ridicules*, sc. 6.

FALSE COUNT, OR A NEW WAY TO PLAY AN OLD GAME, THE, (1682) by Behn. The Isabella-Quillon action was suggested by *Les Précieuses Ridicules*. The only point where Quillon directly imitates Mascarille is in offering to show a wound : act ii. (p. 130 f.) is taken from *Les Précieuses Ridicules*, sc. 11.

FARRIER MADE PHYSICIAN, THE. See *The Dumb Lady*.

FEIGNED INNOCENCE, THE. See *Sir Martin Mar-All*.

FEMALE VIRTUOSOES, THE, (1693) by Wright. (1) The main action is a close adaptation of *Les Femmes Savantes*. (2) A minor action is spun about Witless: act i. (pp. 5–7) was suggested by *Monsieur de Pourceaugnac*, i. 3 ; act ii. (p. 13 ff.) is translated from *Le Malade Imaginaire*, ii. 5, 6 (two-thirds) ; act iv. (p. 34 f.) is adapted from *Monsieur de Pourceaugnac*,

ii. 6 ; act iv. (p. 38 ff.) is adapted and expanded from *Les Fourberies de Scapin*, ii. 6 ; act iv. (p. 39 ff.) was suggested by *Le Mariage Forcé*, sc. 9 ; act v. (p. 44 ff.) is adapted from *Monsieur de Pourceaugnac*, iii. 6.

FRENCH PURITAN, THE. See *Tartuffe*.

GENTLEMAN DANCING MASTER, THE, (1671) by Wycherley. The conception of Paris owes something to Sganarelle in *L'École des Maris*.

HUMORISTS, THE, (1670) by Shadwell. The courting of Theodosia by Crazy, Brisk, and Drybob is a reminiscence of *Le Misanthrope*, where Célimène is courted by Acaste, Clitandre, and Oronte.

IMPERTINENTS, THE. See *The Sullen Lovers*.

IT CANNOT BE. See *Sir Courtly Nice*.

KIND KEEPER, THE. See *Limberham*.

LIBERTINE, THE, (1676) by Shadwell. The play is an adaptation of *Le Nouveau Festin de Pierre* by Rosimond. The only scenes that may have been suggested by Molière are: act iii. (p. 146 f., Enter Don Lopez and Don Antonio . . . Enter Don John and Jacomo), from *Don Juan*, iii. 2 (end), 3 ; and act iii. (p. 147 ff., Enter Leonora, . . . Exeunt), from *Don Juan*, iv. 6.

LIMBERHAM, OR THE KIND KEEPER, (1678) by Dryden. Mrs. Saintly is a free adaptation of Tartuffe. Brainsick = Lisandre in *Les Fâcheux:* act iii. 1 (p. 62) is from *Les Fâcheux*, i. 3.

LONDON CUCKOLDS, THE, (1682) by Ravenscroft.
Act ii. (p. 22 ff.) was suggested by *L'École des Femmes*,
ii. 5. Wiseacre = Arnolphe ; Peggy = Agnès.

LOVE AND A BOTTLE (1698–9) by Farquhar. The conception of Mockmode is drawn from Monsieur Jourdain (*e.g.*, cf. act ii. 2, p. 38 ff., and *Le Bourgeois
Gentilhomme*, ii. 2) and from Monsieur de Pourceaugnac (*e.g.*, cf. act iii. 2, p. 69 ff., and *Monsieur de
Pourceaugnac*, i. 4).

LOVE FOR LOVE (1695) by Congreve. (1) The out-
line for the plot was suggested by *L'Avare*. Cf. *ante*,
p. 197 f. (2) Act i. 1 (p. 205 ff.) is adapted from
Don Juan, iv. 3 ; act ii. 2 (p. 231 f.) was suggested
by *Le Misanthrope*, iii. 4 ; act iv. 3 (p. 285 f.) was
suggested probably by *L'Étourdi*, iii. 4 (opening).
Sir Sampson was suggested by Harpagon.

LOVE IN A NUNNERY. See *The Assignation*.

LOVE IN A TUB. See *The Comical Revenge*.

LOVE IN A WOOD, OR ST. JAMES'S PARK, (1671) by
Wycherley. The use Dapperwit makes of Sir Simon
was suggested by the relation of Horace and Arnolphe
in *L'École des Femmes*. Act iii. 2 (p. 65 ff.) is adapted
freely from *L'École des Maris*, ii. 3, 4. Act v. 1
was suggested by *L'École des Femmes*, v. 3.

The attitude of Gripe to his daughter and her running
away with Dapperwit was suggested by the character
and fate of Sganarelle in *L'École des Maris*.

LOVE'S CONTRIVANCE (1703) by Centlivre. The play
has a very cleverly constructed intrigue based on *Le*

Médecin malgré lui and *Le Mariage Forcé*, in which
appear, with few changes, translations of : *Le
Mariage Forcé*, sc. 1–5, 8 ; *Le Médecin malgré lui*,
i. Suggestions are taken from *Sganarelle*, sc. 1, 2,
and *Le Médecin malgré lui*, ii. 4.

LOVES OF MARS AND VENUS, THE, (pub. 1696) by
Motteux. No indebtedness to Molière in spite of
assertion to the contrary.

LOVE TRIUMPHANT, OR NATURE WILL PREVAIL, (1694)
by Dryden. Act i. 1 (p. 397) was suggested by
Monsieur de Pourceaugnac, ii. 6. Act v. 1 (p. 458 ff.)
was suggested by *Monsieur de Pourceaugnac*, ii. 8.
Sancho is a reminiscence of Lélie in *L'Étourdi*.

MAMAMOUCHI, OR THE CITIZEN TURNED GENTLEMAN,
(1671) by Ravenscroft. Cf. *ante*, p. 103 ff.

MAN OF MODE, OR SIR FOPLING FLUTTER, THE, (1676)
by Etheredge. Act iii. 2 (p. 295 ff.) is adapted from
Les Précieuses Ridicules, sc. 9. Act iv. 1 (p. 327 f.)
and 2 (p. 338 f.) were suggested by *Les Précieuses
Ridicules*, sc. 9 (another passage in the scene). Cf.
ante, p. 136 ff.
For the character of Sir Fopling, cf. *ante*, p. 135 ff.

MARRIED BEAU, OR THE CURIOUS IMPERTINENT, THE,
(1694) by Crowne. Act ii. (p. 272 f.) is a reminiscence of *Les Précieuses Ridicules*, sc. 9.

MARRIAGE À LA MODE (1672) by Dryden. Melantha
is an adaptation from Molière's several paintings of
preciosity.

METAMORPHOSIS, OR THE OLD LOVER OUTWITTED, THE, (1704) by Corey. The play owes nothing to Molière. Cf. *ante*, p. 81.

MISER, THE, (1671) by Shadwell. The main plot is almost a translation of *L'Avare*. But about forty per cent of the play is taken up with the added characters, Timothy Squeeze, Lettice, Joyce, Rant, and Hazard, in scenes from London low life. Anselme of the original does not appear. His will is executed by his son. The plan proposed by Frosine in *L'Avare*, iv. 1, is carried out in action.

MISTAKE, THE, (1705) by Vanbrugh. The play is a translation for the stage of *Le Dépit Amoureux*.

MOCK ASTROLOGER, THE. See *An Evening's Love*.

MODISH WIFE, THE. See *Tom Essence*.

MULBERRY GARDEN, THE, (1668) by Sedley. Act i. (p. 35 ff.) is adapted from *L'École des Maris*, i. 1. No borrowing occurs in the remainder of the play. Forecast (= Sganarelle) and Everyoung (= Ariste) continue through the play. Each has two daughters in place of one ward.

NATURE WILL PREVAIL. See *Love Triumphant*.

NEW WAY TO PLAY AN OLD GAME, A. See *The False Count*.

OLD BACHELOR, THE, (1693) by Congreve. Act ii. (p. 21 ff.) is freely adapted from *Les Fourberies de Scapin*, ii. 7 (cf. the opening of each), with a suggestion from *Monsieur de Pourceaugnac*, i. 4. Act ii.

(p. 28 f.) was suggested by *Les Femmes Savantes*, i. 1. Act iii. 2 (p. 41 f.) is a reminiscence of *George Dandin*, ii. 1. Act iv. 6 (p. 67 f.) is freely adapted from *George Dandin*, ii. 8, with a suggestion from *L'École des Maris*, ii. 9.

The conception of Heartwell owes something to Sganarelle : *e.g.*, cf. *Le Mariage Forcé*, sc. 1, and *The Old Bachelor*, i. (p. 15). Araminta and Belinda show reminiscences of Molière's *précieuses*.

OLD LOVER OUTWITTED, THE. See *The Metamorphosis*.

PLAIN DEALER, THE, (1774) by Wycherley. (1) The play is an adaptation of *Le Misanthrope:* act i. 1 (p. 382 ff.) is adapted from *Le Misanthrope*, i. 1 (first half); act ii. 1 (p. 400 ff.) is adapted from *Le Misanthrope*, ii. 4 ; act iv. 2 is adapted from *Le Misanthrope*, iii. 1, and v. 4. (2) Act ii. 1 (p. 407 ff.) is adapted from *La Critique de l'École des Femmes*. Manly = Alceste ; Freeman = Philinte ; Olivia = Célimène ; Eliza = Éliante ; Novel and Plausible = Acaste and Clitandre.

PLAYHOUSE TO BE LET, THE, (1663) by Davenant. Act ii. is a translation of *Sganarelle*, scenes 7, 12, 13, being omitted. Cf. *ante*, p. 79.

PSYCHE (1674) by Shadwell. The opera is an adaptation of *Psyché:* act i. is composed of selected portions of the prologue and *Psyché*, i. without reference to their order in the original ; in act ii. the first two-thirds is composed of the rest of *Psyché*, i. and the first *intermède ;* the last third, of *Psyché*, ii. condensed; acts iii.–v. are paraphrased with some shortening from *Psyché,* iii.–v.

RELAPSE, OR VIRTUE IN DANGER, THE, (1696) by Vanbrugh. Act i. 3 is a free adaptation from *Le Bourgeois Gentilhomme,* ii. 5. Sir Tunbelly and Hoyden are a reflection of Sganarelle and Isabelle in *L'École des Maris,* probably through *The Country Wife.*

ST. JAMES'S PARK. See *Love in a Wood.*

SCARAMOUCH (1677) by Ravenscroft. (1) The main plot is a close adaptation of *Les Fourberies de Scapin.* (2) The subplot is a close adaptation of *Le Mariage Forcé.* (3) Act i. (pp. 2–5) is adapted from *Le Bourgeois Gentilhomme,* ii. 2, 3 ; act i. (p. 5 f.) was suggested by *Le Bourgeois Gentilhomme,* ii. 4 (opening) ; act ii. (p. 30 ff.) is translated from *Le Bourgeois Gentilhomme,* ii. 4 (first half). Act iv. (p. 58 ff.) was suggested by *Monsieur de Pourceaugnac,* ii. 3.

SCOWRERS, THE, (1691) by Shadwell. The relation of Eugenia and her governess Priscilla is a reflection of the *motif* of *L'École des Maris.*

SIR COURTLY NICE, OR IT CANNOT BE, (1685) by Crowne. Act v. (p. 340 f.) was suggested by *Les Précieuses Ridicules,* sc. 9. Act v. (p. 342 ff.) was suggested by *Les Femmes Savantes,* i. 4.

Lord Bellguard is a reminiscence of Orgon in *Le Tartuffe.*

SIR FOPLING FLUTTER. See *The Man of Mode.*

Sir Martin Mar-All, or the Feigned Innocence, (1667) by Dryden. (1) The play is an adaptation of *L'Étourdi*. Acts iii. (largely), iv., v., are adapted from *L'Étourdi*, ii., iii., iv. Acts i., ii., are adapted from Quinault's *L'Amant Indiscret*, i., iv. (2) Act v. (p. 73 ff.) and a subplot are apparently original with Dryden.

Sir Patient Fancy (1678) by Behn. (1) The Wittmore-Fancy and Lodwick-Isabella actions are adapted from *Le Malade Imaginaire*. (2) The Leander-Lucretia action is developed from hints in *Monsieur de Pourceaugnac*, with adaptation (v. pp. 89–96) of *L'Amour Médecin*, ii. 2–5. (3) The adaptation as a whole is ingeniously managed to produce a comedy of intrigue. There is not much paraphrase.

Sir Salomon, or the Cautious Coxcomb, (1669–70) by Caryll. The Sir Salomon action is a close adaptation of *L'École des Femmes*. The Wary action is constructed as an obverse to it.

Sir Salomon = Sganarelle ; Ralph and Alice = Alain and Georgette; Betty = Agnès; Peregreen = Horace. Wary = Chrysalde. Julia (his daughter), Mr. Single (Sir Salomon's son), and Sir Arthur Addel are added.

Soldier's Fortune, The, (1681) by Otway. The basis of the main intrigue is *L'École des Maris:* act ii. (p. 394 ff.) is adapted from *L'École des Maris*, ii. 2 ; act ii. (pp. 406–9) is adapted from *L'École des Maris*, ii. 2, 6 ; act iii. (pp. 417–420) was suggested by *L'École des Maris*, ii. 3 ; act iv. (p. 421 ff.) was suggested by *L'École des Maris*, ii. 4, 5. Act ii. (pp. 390–4) was suggested by *Sganarelle*, sc. 9, with use of *L'École des Maris*, ii. 4, 7 (end).

Sir Davy Dunce = Sganarelle; Lady Dunce = Isabelle; Fourbin = Scapin (*Les Fourberies de Scapin*).

SPANISH FRIAR, OR THE DOUBLE DISCOVERY, THE, (1681) by Dryden. Act. i. 2 (p. 430 ff.) is freely adapted from *L'École des Femmes*, i. 4. Act iv. 1 (p. 473 f.) is adapted from *Le Médecin malgré lui*, ii. 5.

SQUIRE OF ALSATIA, THE, (1688) by Shadwell. The basis of the play is *L'École des Maris*. Act iv. (p. 73) is adapted from *L'Avare*, i. 5.

Sir William Belfond is a reminiscence of Harpagon in *L'Avare*. The conception also owes something to Sganarelle of *L'École des Maris*. Sir Edward = Ariste ; Belfond Senior and Junior = Isabelle and Léonor.

SQUIRE TRELOOBY (1704) by Congreve, Walsh, and Vanbrugh. This adaptation of *Monsieur de Pourceaugnac* is not extant.

STAGE BEAUX TOSSED IN A BLANKET, THE, (pub. 1704) by Brown. Act i. is translated with few changes from *La Critique de l'École des Femmes*, sc. 1–5, with a suggestion from scene 7. Act iv. (pp. 56–9) is adapted from *Le Tartuffe*, iv. 5, iii. 3 (praise of lady), and iv. 6.

STOCK JOBBERS, THE. See *The Volunteers*.

SULLEN LOVERS, OR THE IMPERTINENTS, THE, (1668) by Shadwell. The main points in the plot were suggested by *Le Misanthrope*. Act i. contains the following adapted scenes: *Le Misanthrope*, i. 1, 2 ; iii. 1 ; *Les Fâcheux*, i. 3. Act ii. contains : *Les Fâcheux*, ii. 3 ; iii. 3. Act iii. contains : *Les Fâcheux*, ii. 2. Act iv. contains : *Les Fâcheux*, iii. 4 ; *Le Misanthrope*, ii. 4.

Stanford = Alceste, weakened to a mere grumbler ; Célimène suggested Emilia, a second Alceste. Lovel = Philinte, Carolina = Éliante ; Ninny = Oronte ; Lady Vaine = Arsinoé. Woodcock is a combination of Lisandre and Ormin in *Les Fâcheux ;* Huffe is a combination of Dorante and Alcippe ; Sir Positive At-All is a combination of Lisandre and Alcandre in *Les Fâcheux*, and of Acaste in *Le Misanthrope*, and of Pancrace (cf. act iv., p. 87 f., and *Le Mariage Forcé*, sc. 4).

TARTUFFE, OR THE FRENCH PURITAN, (1670) by Medbourne. The play is a translation for the stage of *Le Tartuffe*. The only scenes omitted are iv. 8 (last half), v. 2, v. 4 (last half), v. 7 (last half). For slight changes in plot, see *ante*, p. 85 ff.

TOM ESSENCE, OR THE MODISH WIFE, (1677) by Rawlins. (1) The basis of the play is *Sganarelle*, probably in Davenant's translation, followed pretty closely in the Essence action. (2) The lover of Célie and the girl he has married, merely mentioned in *Sganarelle*, are developed, with the addition of a servant, Laurence, not mentioned at all, to furnish a second (Loveall-Luce) action. (3) A third (Moneylove) action is developed by giving the man corresponding to Gorgibus a young wife, who has a gallant, Stanley, who at one point (ii., pp. 16–18) assumes the disguise of a doctor under the influence of some of Molière's doctor scenes.

TOWN SPARKS, THE.   See *The English Friar*.

TRIP TO THE JUBILEE, A.   See *The Constant Couple*.

TWO SOSIAS, THE.   See *Amphitryon*.

TWIN RIVALS, THE, (1702) by Farquhar.   Act iii. 1 (p. 52 f.) was suggested by *Le Médecin malgré lui*, iii. 2.   Act v. 4 (p. 105 ff.) is freely adapted from *Le Tartuffe*, iv. 5, 6.

VIRTUE IN DANGER.   See *The Relapse*.

VIRTUOSO, THE, (1676) by Shadwell.   The treatment of Clarinda and Miranda shows influence from *L'École des Maris*.   Sir Formal, Sir Samuel, and Snarl are reminiscences of Acaste, Clitandre, and Alceste in *Le Misanthrope*.

VOLUNTEERS, OR THE STOCK JOBBERS, THE, (pub. 1693) by Shadwell.   Teresia owes something to Cathos and Madelon in *Les Précieuses Ridicules*.   Mrs. Hackwell is a reminiscence of Sganarelle in *L'École des Maris*.

WANTON WIFE, THE.   See *The Amorous Widow*.

WAY OF THE WORLD, THE, (1700) by Congreve.   Cf. *ante*, p. 198 f.   Waitwell's disguise was suggested by the plot of *Les Précieuses Ridicules*.
Foible is influenced in conception by Molière's sou-

brettes (*e.g.*, Toinette or Lisette). Mrs. Fainall is a variation of the *motif* of *L'École des Maris*.

WOMAN CAPTAIN, THE, (1680) by Shadwell. Act i. (pp. 357 ff.) was suggested by *L'Avare*, iii. 1. The conduct of Mrs. Gripe is a reflection of the *L'École des Maris motif*. Gripe is a reminiscence of Harpagon in *L'Avare*.

BIBLIOGRAPHY

I. TEXTS

THE following list aims to give the full titles of the books cited in the preceding pages. Where more than one edition is given, it is because of introductory matter having some bearing on the subject. In such cases the edition to which reference is made in the notes is always specified.

BEHN, MRS. APHRA, *The Plays, Histories, and Novels of the ingenious . . . , with Life and Memoirs. Complete in Six Volumes.* London, 1871.

BETTERTON, THOMAS, *The Amorous Widow: or, the Wanton Wife. A Comedy. As it is Perform'd by Her Majesty's Servants. Written by the late Famous Mr. Thomas Betterton. Now first Printed from the Original Copy.* London: Printed in the Year 1710.

[BROWN, THOMAS], *The Stage-Beaux toss'd in a Blanket: or, Hypocrisie Alamode; Expos'd in a True Picture of Jerry —— A Pretending Scourge to the English Stage. A Comedy with a Prologue on Occasional Conformity; being a full Explanation of the Poussin Doctor's Book; and an Epilogue on the Reformers. Spoken at the Theatre-Royal in Drury-Lane.* London, Printed, and Sold by J. Nutt, near Stationers-Hall, 1704.

[CARYLL, JOHN], *Sir Salomon; or, the Cautious Coxcomb, a Comedy. Acted By Their Majesties Servants. By Mr. Caryl.* London, Printed for H. Herringman, and Sold by Jacob Tonson, at the Judges-Head in Chancery-Lane near Fleetstreet, 1691.

CENTLIVRE, MRS. [SUSANNA], *The Dramatic Works of the Celebrated Mrs. Centlivre, with A New Account of her Life. Complete in Three Volumes.* London, 1872.

CONGREVE, WILLIAM, *The Comedies of, with an introduction by G. S. Street. In two volumes.* London, 1895. [In *English Classics*, edited by W. E. Henley.]

CONGREVE, WILLIAM, [*The Complete Plays of.*] *Edited by Alex[ander] Charles Ewald.* New York, —. [In *The Mermaid Series.*] Quotations are from this edition.

[COREY, JOHN], *The Metamorphosis: or, the Old Lover Out-witted. A Farce. As it is now Acted at the New Theatre in Lincolns-Inn-Fields. Written Originally by the Famous Moliere.* London : Printed for Bernard Lintott at the Middle-Temple Gate in Fleetstreet. 1704.

CROWNE, JOHN, *The Dramatic Works of, with prefatory memoir and notes.* Edinburgh and London, 1873–4. [In *Dramatists of the Restoration*, edited by James Maidment and W. H. Logan.]

D'AVENANT, SIR WILLIAM, *The Dramatic Works of, with prefatory memoir and notes.* Edinburgh and

London, 1872–4. [In *Dramatists of the Restoration*, edited by James Maidment and W. H. Logan.]

DODSLEY, ROBERT, *A Select Collection of Old English Plays. Originally published by Robert Dodsley in the year 1744. Fourth Edition, now first chronologically arranged, revised and enlarged with the notes of all the commentators, and new notes by W. Carew Hazlitt.* Volume the fifteenth. London, 1876. [Contains *The Adventures of Five Hours*, by Tuke, and *Historia Histrionica*, by Wright.]

The Dramatic Works of Wycherley, Congreve, Vanbrugh, and Farquhar. With Biographical and Critical Notices by Leigh Hunt. A New Edition. London and New York, 1875

DRYDEN, JOHN, *Essays of, Selected and edited by W. P. Ker. [In two volumes.]* Oxford, 1900.

DRYDEN, JOHN, *The Works of, illustrated with notes, historical, critical, and explanatory, and a life of the author, by Sir Walter Scott, Bart. Revised and corrected by George Saintsbury.* Edinburgh, 1882–1893.

DURFEY, THOMAS, *The Fond Husband: or, the Plotting Sisters. A Comedy as it is acted at the Theatre-Royal in Drury Lane. Written by Tho. Durfey, Gent.* London, 1735.

ETHEREDGE, SIR GEORGE, *The Works of, Plays and Poems. Edited, with critical notes and introduction, by A. Wilson Verity.* London, 1888.

FARQUHAR, GEORGE, *The Dramatic Works of, edited*

*with a life and notes by Alex[ander] Charles Ewald.
In two volumes.* London, 1892.

FOURNEL, VICTOR, *Les Contemporains de Molière.
Recueil de comédies, rares ou peu connues, jouées de
1650 à 1680, avec l'histoire de chaque théâtre, des notes
et notices biographiques, bibliographiques et critiques.*
Paris, 1863–6.

LACY, JOHN, *The Dramatic Works of, with prefatory
memoir and notes.* Edinburgh and London, 1875.
[In *Dramatists of the Restoration*, edited by James
Maidment and W. H. Logan.]

MEDBOURNE, M[ATTHEW], *Tartuffe: or the French
Puritan. A Comedy, Lately Acted at the Theatre
Royal. Written in French by Moliere; and rendered
into English with Much Addition and Advantage, By
M. Medbourne, Servant to his Royal Highness.* London : Printed by H. L. and R. B. for James Magnus
at the Posthouse in Russel-street near the Piazza in
Covent Garden, 1670.

MOLIÈRE, *Œuvres complètes de.* Oxford, 1900. [Reproduces the Despois-Mesnard text in a single
volume.]

MOLIÈRE, *Œuvres de. Nouvelle édition revue sur les plus
anciennes impressions et augmentée des variantes, de
notices, de notes, d'un lexique des mots et locutions
remarquables, de portraits, de fac-simile, etc. Par
MM. Eugène Despois et Paul Mesnard.* Paris, 1873–
1900. [Dans la Collection des Grands Écrivains
de la France.]

MOTTEUX [PIERRE ANTOINE], *The Loves of Mars &
Venus. A Play set to Music, As it is Acted at the
New Theatre, in Little Lincolns Inn-Fields. By His
Majesty's Servants. Written by Mr. Motteux.* Lon-
don, Printed, and are to be sold at the New Theatre,
in Little Lincolns-Inn-Fields. 1696.

OTWAY, THOMAS, [*The Best Plays of.*] *With an Introduction and Notes, by The Hon. Roden Noel.* London and New York, —. [In *The Mermaid Series.*]

OTWAY, THOMAS, *The Works of, consisting of his Plays,
Poems, and Letters. With a Sketch of his Life, enlarged from that written by Dr. Johnson. In two
volumes.* London, 1812. Quotations are from this
edition.

OTWAY, THOMAS, *The Works of, in three volumes. With
Notes, Critical and Explanatory, and a Life of the
Author, By Thomas Thornton, Esq.* London, 1813.

RAVENSCROFT, EDWARD, *The Canterbury Guests; or,
a Bargain Broken. A Comedy. Acted at The Theatre-
Royal. Written by Mr. . . . ,* London, Printed for
Daniel Brown at the Bible without Temple-Barr;
and John Walthoe, at his Shop in Vine-Court,
Middle-Temple, 1695.

RAVENSCROFT, EDWARD, *The Careless Lovers: A Comedy
Acted at the Duke's Theatre. Written by Edward
Ravenscrofts, Gent.* London, Printed for William
Cademan, at the Popes Head in the Lower Walk
in the New Exchange, 1673.

RAVENSCROFT, EDWARD, *The Citizen turn'd Gentleman: a Comedy. Acted at the Duke's Theatre. By Edw. Ravenscroft. Gent.* London, Printed for Thomas Dring, at the White-Lyon next Chancery-Lane end in Fleetstreet, 1672. Quotations are from this edition.

RAVENSCROFT, EDWARD, *The London Cuckolds. A Comedy; As it is Acted at The Duke's Theatre. By Edward Ravenscroft, Gent.* London, Printed for Jos. Hindmarsh at the Sign of the Black-Bull near the Royal-Exchange in Cornhill, Anno Dom., 1682.

RAVENSCROFT, EDWARD, *Mamamouchi, or the Citizen turn'd Gentleman: a Comedy Acted at the Duke's Theatre. By Edw. Ravenscroft. Gent.* London, Printed for Thomas Dring, at the Corner of Chancery-Lane, over against the Inner Temple Gate in Fleetstreet, 1675.

RAVENSCROFT, EDWARD, *Scaramouch a Philosopher, Harlequin a School-Boy, Bravo, Merchant, and Magician. A Comedy After the Italian manner. Acted at the Theatre-Royal. Written by Mr. . . .* Printed for Robert Sollers at the Flying Horse in St. Pauls Church-yard, 1677.

[RAWLINS, THOMAS], *Tom Essence: or, The Modish Wife. A Comedy. As it is Acted at the Duke's Theatre. Licensed, Novemb. the 4th. 1676. Roger L'Estrange.* London, Printed by T. M. for W. Cademan, at the Popes-Head in the Lower Walk of the New-Exchange in the Strand, 1677.

SEDLEY, SIR CHARLES, BART., *The Works of the Honourable, In Prose and Verse. In Two Volumes.*

Containing the Translations of Virgil's Pastorals, the Battle and Government of Bees, &c. With his Speeches, Political Pieces, Poems, Songs and Plays, the greatest Part never printed before, . . . With Memoirs of the Author's Life, Written by an Eminent Hand. London, 1778.

SHADWELL, THOMAS, [*The Best Plays of.*] *Edited, with an Introduction and Notes, by George Saintsbury.* London and New York, ——. [In *The Mermaid Series.*]

SHADWELL, THOMAS, Esq., *The Dramatick Works of; In four volumes.* London, 1720. Quotations are from this edition.

SOUTHERNE, THOMAS, Esq., *Plays written by . . . Now first collected. With An Account of the Life and Writings of the Author.* London, 1774.

[TOMKIS, THOMAS], *Albumazar. A Comedy presented before the Kings Maiesty at Cambridge. By the Gentlemen of Trinity Colledge. Newly revised and corrected by a speciall Hand.* London, Printed by Nicholas Okes, 1634.

TUKE, SIR SAMUEL, *The Adventures of Five Hours.* See Dodsley.

VANBRUGH, SIR JOHN, *Edited by W[illiam] C. Ward. In two volumes.* London, 1893. Quotations are from this edition.

VANBRUGH, SIR JOHN, [*The Select Plays of.*] *Edited, with an Introduction and Notes, by A. E. H. Swaen.*

London and New York, 1896. [In *The Mermaid Series.*]

WRIGHT, THOMAS, *The Female Vertuoso's. A Comedy: As it is Acted at the Queen's Theatre, By their Majesties Servants. Written by Mr. . . .* London, Printed by J. Wilde, for R. Vincent, in Cliffords-Inn-lane, Fleet-street, 1693.

WYCHERLEY, WILLIAM, [*The Complete Plays of.*] *Edited with Introduction and Notes by W. C. Ward.* London and New York, —. [In *The Mermaid Series.*] Quotations are from this edition.

II. GENERAL WORKS AND SPECIAL STUDIES

This bibliography does not embrace all the works consulted in the preparation of the preceding chapters, but only those bearing on some phase of the subject as there treated, chiefly for the purpose of giving full titles of books referred to in the notes. Very few titles for Molière have been included, since the bibliography by Currier and Gay will indicate what has been at my disposal. I have tried to make the titles exact, but not always complete. As in the first section, date and place of publication have been reduced to a uniform style.

ALBRECHT, L., *Dryden's "Sir Martin Mar-all" in Bezug auf seine Quellen.* [Dissertation, Rostock] Rostock, 1906.

ARCHER, WILLIAM, *The Comedies of Congreve.* [In *The Forum*, vol. xliii. New York, 1910.]

[BAKER, DAVID ERSKINE], *The Companion to the Playhouse: or, An Historical Account of all the Dramatic Writers (and their Works) that have appeared in Great Britain and Ireland, from the Commencement of our Theatrical Exhibitions, down to the Present Year 1764. Composed in the Form of a Dictionary, For the more readily turning to any particular Author, or Performance. In Two Volumes.* London : Printed for T. Beckct and P. A. Dehondt, in the Strand ; C. Henderson, at the Royal Exchange ; and T. Davies, in Russel-Street, Covent-Garden. 1764.

BARTOLI, ADOLFO, *Scenari inediti della commedia dell'arte. Contributo alla storia del teatro popolare italiano.* Firenze, 1880. [In *Raccolta di opere inedite o rare di ogni secolo della letteratura italiana.*]

BELJAME, ALEXANDRE, *Le Public et les hommes de lettres en Angleterre au dix-huitième siècle 1660–1744 (Dryden-Addison-Pope). Ouvrage couronné par l'Académie française. Deuxième édition augmentée d'un index.* Paris, 1897.

BELLONI, ANTONIO, *Il Seicento.* Milano,——. [In *Storia letteraria d'Italia scritta da una società di professori.*]

BENNEWITZ, ALEXANDER, *Congreve und Molière. Literar-Historische Untersuchung.* Leipzig, 1890.

BENNEWITZ, ALEXANDER, *Molière's Einfluss auf Congreve.* [Dissertation, Leipzig] Leipzig, 1889.

BOBERTAG, FELIX, *Zu John Dryden.* [In *Englische Studien. Organ für englische Philologie unter Mitberücksichtigung des englischen Unterrichtes auf höheren Schulen.* Herausgegeben von Dr. Eugen Kölbing. IV Band. Heilbronn, 1881.]

BRUNETIÈRE, F[ERDINAND], *Les Époques de la comédie de Molière.* [Dans *la Revue de deux mondes.* lxxvie année — cinquième période. Tome trent-et-unième. Paris, 1906.]

BURGHCLERE, WINIFRED, LADY, *George Villiers, Second Duke of Buckingham. 1628–1687. A Study in the History of the Restoration. With portraits and illustrations.* London, 1903.

[BURNET, GILBERT, BISHOP OF SALISBURY], *Some Passages of the Life and Death of the Right Honourable John, Earl of Rochester. Reprinted in facsimile from the Edition of* 1680. *With an Introductory Preface by Lord Ronald Gower.* London, 1875.

CANFIELD, DOROTHEA FRANCES, *Corneille and Racine in England. A Study of the English Translations of the two Corneilles and Racine, with especial Reference to their Presentation on the English Stage.* [Dissertation, Columbia] New York, 1904.

CHASE, LEWIS NATHANIEL, *The English Heroic Play.* [Dissertation, Columbia] New York, 1903.

CHARLANNE, LOUIS, *L'Influence française en Angleterre au xviie siècle. La vie sociale — la vie littéraire. Étude sur les relations sociales et littéraires de la*

France et de l'Angleterre surtout dans la seconde moitié du XVIIe siècle. Paris, 1906.

CHATFIELD-TAYLOR, H[OBART] C[HATFIELD], *Molière, a Biography. With an introduction by Thomas Frederick Crane. Illustrations by JoB.* New York, 1906.

CIBBER, COLLEY, *An Apology for the Life of, written by himself. A New Edition with Notes and Supplement by Robert W. Lowe. With twenty-six mezzotint portraits by R. B. Parkes, and eighteen etchings by Adolphe Lalauze. In two volumes.* London, 1889.

COLLINS, GEORGE STUART, *Dryden's Dramatic Theory and Praxis.* [Dissertation, Leipzig] Leipzig-Reudnitz, 1802.

COLLINS, JOHN CHURTON, *Essays and Studies.* London, 1895.

CORRADINO, CORRADO, *Il Secentismo e l'Adone del cavalier Marino. Considerazione critiche.* Torino, 1880.

COURTHOPE, W[ILLIAM] J[OHN], *A History of English Poetry. Vol. IV. Development and Decline of the Poetic Drama: Influence of the Court and the People.* London, 1903.

CRULL, FRANZ, *Thomas Shadwell's (John Ozell's) und Henry Fielding's Comoedien "The Miser" in ihrem Verhältnis unter einander und zu ihrer gemeinsamen Quelle.* [Dissertation, Rostock] Rostock, 1899.

CUNNINGHAM, PETER, *The Story of Nell Gwyn and the Sayings of Charles II. Related and collected by*

Peter Cunningham, with the author's latest corrections, portraits and all the original illustrations. Edited, with introduction, additional notes, and a life of the author, by Henry B. Wheatley. London, 1896. [In *Memoir Library.*]

CURRIER and GAY, *Catalogue of the Molière Collection in Harvard College Library. Acquired chiefly from the library of the late Ferdinand Bôcher. Compiled by Thomas Franklin Currier and Ernest Lewis Gay.* Cambridge, Mass. 1906. [No. 57 in *Bibliographical Contributions*, edited by William Coolidge Lane.]

DAMETZ, MAX, *John Vanbrughs Leben und Werke.* Wien und Leipzig, 1898. [In *Wiener Beiträge zur englischen Philologie.* . . . Herausgegeben von Dr. J. Schipper. VII Band.]

DEKKER, THOMAS, *The Gull's Horn-book, edited by R. B. McKerrow.* London, 1904. [In *The King's Library,* edited by Professor Gollancz.]

[DENNIS, JOHN], *A Defence of Sir Fopling Flutter, a Comedy written by Sir George Etheridge. In which defence is shewn, That Sir Fopling, that merry Knight, was rightly compos'd by the Knight his Father, to answer the Ends of Comedy; and that he has been barbarously and scurrilously attack'd by the Knight his Brother, in the 65th Spectator. By which it appears, That the latter Knight knows nothing of the Nature of Comedy.* London: Printed for T. Warner, at the Black Boy in Pater-noster Row. 1722.

DENNIS, [JOHN], *Some Remarkable Passages of the Life of Mr. Wycherley.* [In] *A New Collection of Miscellanies in Prose and Verse*, [by Richardson Pack]. London : Printed for E. Curll, in the Strand. 1725.

DESPOIS, EUGÈNE, *Le Théâtre français sous Louis XIV. Quatrième édition.* Paris, 1894.

DIBDIN, [CHARLES], *A Complete History of the English Stage. Introduced by a comparative and comprehensive review of the Asiatic, the Grecian, the Roman, the Spanish, the Italian, the Portugese, the German, the French, and Other Theatres, and involving Biographical Tracts and Anecdotes, instructive and amusing, concerning a prodigious number of Authors, Composers, Painters, Actors, Singers, and Patrons of Dramatic Productions in all countries. The whole written with the assistance of interesting documents, collected in the course of five and thirty years.* London, [1800].

Dictionary of National Biography. Edited by Leslie Stephen and Sidney Lee. London, 1885–1904.

DORAN, [JOHN], *"Their Majesties Servants" Annals of the English Stage from Thomas Betterton to Edmund Kean. Edited and Revised by Robert W. Lowe. With fifty copperplate portraits and eighty wood engravings. In three volumes.* London, 1888.

DOWNES, JOHN, *Roscius Anglicanus, or, an Historical Review of the Stage From 1660 to 1706. A Fac-simile Reprint of the Rare Original of 1708. With an Historical Preface by Joseph Knight.* London, 1886.

ELTON, OLIVER, *The Augustan Ages.* New York, 1899. [In *Periods of European Literature*, edited by Professor Saintsbury.]

ERICHSEN, ASMUS, *Thomas Shadwell's Komödie "The Sullen Lovers" in ihrem Verhältnis zu Molière's "Le Misanthrope" und "Les Fâcheux."* [Dissertation, Kiel] Flensburg, 1906.

FERCHLANDT, HANS, *Molière's Misanthrop und seine englische Nachahmungen.* [Dissertation, Halle] Halle, 1907.

FISCHER, R[UDOLF], *Thomas Middleton. Eine literarhistorische Skizze.* [In *Festschrift zum viii. allgemeinen deutschen Neuphilologentage in Wien Pfingsten 1898. Verfasst von Mitgliedern der Österreichischen Universitäten und des wiener neuphololologischen Vereins.* Herausgegeben von J. Schipper. Wien und Leipzig, 1898.]

FITZGERALD, PERCY [HETHRINGTON], *A New History of the English Stage from the Restoration to the Liberty of the Theatres, in Connection with the Patent Houses, From Original Papers in the Lord Chamberlain's Office, the State Paper Office, and other Sources. In two volumes.* London, 1882.

FLAMINI, FRANCESCO, *Il Cinquecento.* Milano, ——. [In *Storia letteraria d'Italia scritta da una società di professori.*]

FLEAY, FREDERICK GARD, *A Chronicle History of the London Stage* (1559–1642). London, 1890.

FOURNEL, VICTOR, *Le Théâtre au XVII⁰ siècle. La Comédie.* Paris, 1892.

GARNETT, R[ICHARD], *The Age of Dryden.* London, 1903. [In *Handbooks of English Literature,* edited by Professor Hales.]

[GENEST, JOHN], *Some Account of the English Stage, from the Restoration in 1660 to 1830. In ten volumes.* Bath, 1832.

[GILDON, CHARLES], *The Life of Mr. Thomas Betterton, The Late Eminent Tragedian. Wherein The Action and Utterance of the Stage, Bar, and Pulpit, are distinctly consider'd. With the Judgment of the late Ingenious Monsieur de St. Evremond, upon the Italian and French Music and Opera's; in a Letter to the Duke of Buckingham. To which is added, The Amorous Widow, or the Wanton Wife. A Comedy. Written by Mr. Betterton. Now first printed from the Original Copy.* London : Printed for Robert Gosling, at the Mitre, near the Inner-Temple Gate in Fleetstreet. 1710.

[GILDON, CHARLES], *The Lives and Characters of the English Dramatic Poets. Also An Exact Account of all the Plays that were ever yet Printed in the English Tongue; their Double Titles, the Places where Acted, the Dates when Printed, and the Persons to whom Dedicated; with Remarks and Observations on most of the said Plays. First begun by Mr. Langbain, improv'd and continued down to this Time, by a Careful Hand.* London : Printed for Tho. Leigh at the

Peacock against St. Dunstan's-Church, and William Turner at the White Horse, without Temple-Bar. [1699.]

GOSSE, EDMUND, *A History of Eighteenth Century Literature* (1660–1780). London, 1889.

GOSSE, EDMUND, *Life of William Congreve*. London, 1888.

GOSSE, EDMUND W[ILLIAM], *Seventeenth Century Studies. A Contribution to the History of English Poetry*. London, 1883.

GRISY, A[MBROISE] DE, *Étude sur Thomas Otway*. Paris, 1868.

GRISY, A[MBROISE] DE, *Histoire de la comédie anglaise au dix-septième siècle* (1672–1707). Paris, 1878.

GROSSE, WILHELM, *John Crowne's Komödien und burleske Dichtung*. [Dissertation, Leipzig] Lucka, 1903.

HALLBAUER, O., *George Farquhar's life and works. Beilage zum Program des herzoglichen Gymnasiums zu Holzminden*. Holzminden, 1880.

HARTMANN, CARL, *Einfluss Molière's auf Dryden's Komisch-Dramatische Dichtungen*. [Dissertation, Leipzig] Leipzig, 1885.

HARVEY-JELLIE, W., *Les Sources du théâtre anglais à l'époque de la Restauration*. [Dissertation, Paris] Paris, 1906.

HATCHER, ORIE LATHAM, *John Fletcher. A Study in Dramatic Method*. [Dissertation, Chicago] Chicago, 1905.

HAZLITT, WILLIAM, *The Collected Works of. Edited by A. R. Waller and Arnold Glover, with an introduction by W. E. Henley.* London and New York, 1902–4.

HETTNER, HERMANN, *Geschichte der englischen Literatur von der Wiederherstellung des Königthums bis in die zweite Hälfte des achzehnten Jahrhunderts. 1660–1770. Fünfte verbesserte Auflage.* Braunschweig, 1894.

HOHRMANN, FRIEDRICH, *Das Verhältniss Susanna Centlivre's zu Molière und Regnard.* [In *Zeitschrift für vergleichende Litteraturgeschichte.* Herausgegeben von Dr. Max Koch. Vierzehnter Band. Berlin, 1901.]

HOLZHAUSEN, P[AUL], *Dryden's Heroisches Drama.* [In *Englische Studien*, xiii., xv., xvi. Heilbronn, 1889, und Leipzig, 1891, 1892.]

HUSZÁR, GUILLAUME, *Molière et l'Espagne.* Paris, 1907. [II. in *Études critiques de littérature comparée.*]

[HUTCHINSON], LUCY [APSLEY], *Memoirs of the Life of Colonel Hutchinson. Governor of Nottingham, by his Widow Lucy. Edited from the original manuscript by the Rev. Julius Hutchinson. To which are added the letters of Colonel Hutchinson and other papers. Revised with additional notes by C. H. Firth. With ten etched portraits of eminent personages. In two volumes.* London, 1885.

[JACOB, GILES], *The Poetical Register: or, the Lives and Characters of all the English Poets. With an Account of their Writings. Adorned with curious Sculptures engraven by the best Masters.* [*In two volumes.*]

London : Printed, and Sold by A. Bettesworth,
W. Taylor, and J. Batley, in Paternoster Row;
. . . 1723.

JOHNSON, SAMUEL, *Lives of the English Poets, edited by
George Birbeck Hill, . . . with brief memoir of Dr.
Birbeck Hill, by his nephew, Harold Spencer Scott.
In three volumes.* Oxford, 1905.

KERBY, W. MOSELEY, *Molière and the Restoration
Comedy in England.* [Dissertation, Rennes] [Pri-
vately printed, 1907.]

KLETTE, JOHANNES, *William Wycherley's Leben und
dramatische Werke.* [Dissertation, Münster] Münster,
1883.

KRAUSE, HUGO, *Wycherley und seine französische
Quellen.* [Dissertation, Halle] Halle, 1883.

LAMB, CHARLES, *The Works of Charles and Mary Lamb,
edited by E. V. Lucas.* New York and London,
1903–1905.

LANGBAINE, GERARD, *An Account of the English Dramatick Poets. Or, Some Observations And Remarks
On the Lives and Writings, of all those that have Pub-
lish'd either Comedies, Tragedies, Tragi-Comedies,
Pastorals, Masques, Interludes, Farces, or Opera's in
the English Tongue.* Oxford, Printed by L. L. for
George West, and Henry Clements. An. Dom.
1691.

LANSON, GUSTAVE, *Molière et la farce.* [Dans *la Revue
de Paris.* Huitième année. Tome troisième. Mai
–juin 1901.]

LARROUMET, GUSTAVE, *La Comédie de Molière.*
L'Auteur et le milieu. Sixième édition. Paris, 1903.

LAUN, HENRI VAN, *The Dramatic Works of Molière*
rendered into English. With a prefatory memoir,
introductory notices, appendices and notes. Edinburgh, 1875–6.

LAVISSE, ERNEST, *Histoire de France depuis les origines*
jusqu'à la Revolution. Publié avec la collaboration
de M. Bayet, Bloch, . . . Tome septième. I.
Louis XIV. La Fronde. Le Roi. Colbert. (1643–
1685) par E. Lavisse. Paris, 1906. II. *Louis*
XIV. La Religion. Les Lettres et les arts. La
Guerre. (1643–1685) par E. Lavisse. Paris, 1906.

The Life and Times of that Excellent and Renowned
Actor Thomas Betterton, Of the Duke's and United
Companies, at the Theatres in Portugal Street, Dorset
Gardens, Drury Lane, &c., during the latter half of
the seventeenth century. With such Notices of the
Stage and English History, before and after the Res-
toration, as serve generally to illustrate the subject.
By the Author and Editor of the Lives of "Mrs. Abing-
don," "James Quin," etc., etc. London, 1888.

LISSNER, MAX, *Sir Charles Sedley's Leben und Werke.*
[In *Anglia. Zeitschrift für englische Philologie. . . .*
Band 27. Neue Folge Band 16. Halle, 1905.]

LIVET, CH[ARLES]-L[OUIS], *Précieux et précieuses.*
Caractères et mœurs littéraires du xviie siècle. Trois-
ième édition. Paris, 1895.

LOHR, ANTON, *Richard Flecknoe. Eine literarhis-*

torische Untersuchung. Leipzig, 1905. [In *Münchener Beiträge zur romanischen und englischen Philologie.* Herausgegeben von H. Breymann und J. Schick. XXXIII.]

LOUNSBURY, THOMAS R[AYNESFORD], *Shakespeare as a Dramatic Artist, with an account of his reputation at various periods.* New York and London, 1901.

LOWE, ROBERT W[ILLIAM], *A Bibliographical Account of English Theatrical Literature from the earliest times to the present day.* London, 1888.

LOWE, ROBERT W[ILLIAM], *Thomas Betterton.* New York, 1891.

[MACAULAY, THOMAS BABINGTON], *The Works of Lord Macaulay Complete. Edited by his sister, Lady Trevelyan. In eight volumes.* London, 1879.

MALONE, EDMOND, *The Critical and Miscellaneous Prose Works of John Dryden, now first collected: with notes and illustrations; an account of the life and writings of the author, grounded on original and authentick documents; and a collection of his letters, the greater part of which has never before been published.* London, 1800.

MARTINENCHE, E[RNEST], *Molière et le théâtre espagnol.* Paris, 1906.

[MATTHEWS, BRANDER], *Molière.* [In *The Edinburgh Review.* Vol. CCXI, No. 431. January, 1910.]

MEINDL, VINCENZ, *Sir George Etheredge, sein Leben, seine Zeit und seine Dramen.* Wien und Leipzig,

1901. [In *Wiener Beiträge zur englischen Philologie.*
. . . Herausgegeben von Dr. J. Schipper. XIV
Band.]

MEREDITH, GEORGE, *An Essay on Comedy and the Uses
of the Comic Spirit. Second edition.* Westminster,
1898.

MOLAND, LOUIS, *Molière et la comédie italienne. Ouvrage illustré de vingt vignettes représentant les princi-
paux types du théâtre italien. Deuxième édition.*
Paris, 1867.

*Moliériste, Le, Revue mensuelle, publiée avec le concours
de MM:* . . . par Georges Monval. Paris, 1879–
1888.

OHLSEN, FRIEDR[ICH], *Dryden as Dramatist and Critic.
Jahres-Bericht des Realgymnasiums und der Real-
schule zu Altona* . . . Altona, 1883.

OHNSORG, RICHARD, *John Lacy's "Dumb Lady," Mrs.
Susanna Centlivre's "Love's Contrivance," und Henry
Fielding's "Mock Doctor" in ihrem Verhältnis zu
einander und zu ihrer gemeinschaftlichen Quelle.*
[Dissertation, Rostock] Hamburg, 1900.

OTT, PHILIPP, *Über das Verhältniss des Lustspiel-
Dichters Dryden zur gleichzeitigen französischen Komödie, insbesondere zu Molière. Programm der Kgl.
Bayer. Studien-Anstalt Landshut für das Schuljahr
1887–8.*

PEPYS, SAMUEL, *The Diary of* . . . *Clerk of the Acts
and Secretary to the Admiralty. Completely transcribed by the late Rev. Mynors Bright, from the short-*

hand manuscript in the Pepysian Library, Magdalene College, Cambridge. With Lord Braybrooke's Notes. Edited with additions by Henry B. Wheatley. London, 1893–9.

PETIT DE JULLEVILLE, L[OUIS], *Histoire de la langue et de la littérature française des origines à* 1900. Publiée sous la direction de . . . Paris, 1896–9.

PLÜCKHAHN, EDMUND, *Die Bearbeitung ausländischer Stoffe im englischen Drama am Ende des* 17. *Jahrhunderts dargelegt an Sir Charles Sedley's: The Mulberry Garden und Bellamira or the Mistress.* [Dissertation, Rostock] [Hamburg, 1904].

PRYNNE, WILLIAM, *Histrio-mastix. The Players Scvrge, or, Actors Tragœdie, Divided into Two Parts.* . . . London, Printed by E. A. and W. I. for Michael Sparke, and are to be sold at the Blue Bible, in Greene Arbour, in little Old Bayly. 1633.

QUAAS, CURT, *William Wycherley als Mensch und Dichter. Ein Beitrag zur englischen Literaturgeschichte des Restaurationszeitalters.* [Dissertation, Rostock] Rostock, 1907.

REIHMANN, OSKAR, *Thomas Shadwells Tragödie "The Libertine" und ihr Verhältnis zu den vorausgehenden Bearbeitungen der Don Juan-Sage.* [Dissertation, Leipzig] Leipzig, 1904.

REINHARDTSTOETTNER, KARL VON, *Plautus. Spätere Bearbeitungen plautinischer Lustspiele. Ein Beitrag zur vergleichenden Litteraturgeschichte.* Leipzig, 1886.

RIEDEL, OTTO, *Dryden's influence on the dramatical literature of England.* [Dissertation, Rostock] Crossen, 1868.

ROSBUND, MAX, *Dryden als Shakspeare-Bearbeiter.* [Dissertation, Halle] Halle, 1882.

SAINTSBURY, G[EORGE], *Dryden.* New York, —. [In *English Men of Letters*]

SANDMANN, PAUL, *Molières "École des Femmes" und Wycherleys "Country Wife."* [In *Archiv für das Studium der neureren Sprachen und Litteraturen.* Herausgegeben von Ludwig Herrig. XXXVIII. Jahrgang, 72 Band. Braunschweig, 1884.]

SCHERILLO, MICHELE, *La Commedia dell' arte in Italia. Studi e profili.* Torino, 1884.

SCHMID, D., *George Farquhar, sein Leben und seine Original-Dramen.* Wien und Leipzig, 1904. [In *Wiener Beiträge zur englischen Philologie* . . . Herausgegeben von Dr. J. Schipper. XVIII. Band.]

SCHMID, D., *William Congreve, sein Leben und seine Lustspiele.* Wien und Leipzig, 1897. [In *Wiener Beiträge zur englischen Philologie* . . . Herausgegeben von Dr. J. Schipper. VI. Band.]

SCHRÖDER, EDWIN, *Dryden's letztes Drama. Love Triumphant or Nature will Prevail.* [Dissertation, Rostock] Rostock, 1905.

SEIBT, ROBERT, *Die Komödien der Mrs. Centlivre.* [In *Anglia. Zeitschrift für englische Philologie.* Band

XXXII. Neue Folge Band XX. und Band XXXIII. Neue Folge Band XXI. Halle, 1909–1910.]

SHERWOOD, MARGARET, *Dryden's Dramatic Theory and Practice.* [Dissertation, Yale] Boston, 1898 [*Yale Studies in English,* IV.]

SMITH, WINIFRED, *Italian and Elizabethan Comedy.* [In *Modern Philology,* volume five, 1907–8.]

SPENCE, JOSEPH, *Anecdotes, Observations, and Characters, of Books and Men. Collected from the conversation of Mr. Pope, and other eminent persons of his time. With notes, and a life of the author. By Samuel Weller Singer. Second Edition.* London, 1858.

STEIGER, AUGUST, *Thomas Shadwell's "Libertine." A Complementary Study to the Don Juan-literature.* [In *Untersuchungen zur neueren Sprach- und Literaturgeschichte.* Herausgegeben von Professor Dr. Oskar F. Walzel. 5. Heft.] Bern, 1904.

SYLE, L[OUIS] DUPONT, *Essays in Dramatic Criticism, with Impressions of Some Modern Plays.* New York, [1898].

TAINE, H[YPPOLITE], *Histoire de la littérature anglaise. Huitième édition revue et augmentée d'un index biographique et bibliographique.* Paris, 1892.

THORNDIKE, ASHLEY H., *Tragedy.* Boston and New York, [1908]. [In *The Types of English Literature,* under the general editorship of Professor William A. Neilson.]

THOMPSON, ELBERT N. S., *The Controversy between the*

Puritans and the Stage. [Dissertation, Yale] New York, 1903. [*Yale Studies in English,* XX.]

WARD, ADOLPHUS WILLIAM, *A History of English Dramatic Literature to the Death of Queen Anne. New and revised edition* [*in three volumes*]. London and New York, 1899.

WERNICKE, ARTHUR, *Das Verhältnis von John Lacys "The Dumb Lady, or the Farrier made Physician" an Molière's "Le Médecin malgré lui" und "L'Amour médecin."* [Dissertation, Halle] Halle, 1903.

WESELMANN, FRANZ, *Dryden als Kritiker.* [Dissertation, Göttingen] Mülheim, 1893.

WHINCOP, THOMAS, *Scanderbeg: or, Love and Liberty. A Tragedy. Written by the late Thomas Whincop, Esq. To which are added A List of all the Dramatic Authors, with some Account of their Lives; and of all the Dramatic Pieces ever published in the English Language, to the Year* 1747. London : Printed for W. Reeve at Shakspear's Head, Serjeant's-Inn-Gate, in Fleet-street. 1747.

WINDSOR, ARTHUR LLOYD, *Ethica: or, Characteristics of Men, Manners, and Books.* London, 1860.

[WRIGHT, JAMES], *Historia Histrionica. An Historical Account of the English-Stage; showing the Ancient Uses, Improvement, and Perfection of Dramatic Representations, in this Nation. In a Dialogue, of Plays and Players.* London, Printed by G. Croom, for William Haws, at the Rose in Ludgate-Street. 1699. [In Hazlitt's Dodsley, XV.]

WÜLLENWEBER, ALBERT, *Mrs. Centlivre's Lustspiel "Love's Contrivance" und seine Quellen.* [Dissertation, Halle] Halle, 1900.

WURZBACH, WOLFGANG VON, *George Etheredge.* [In *Englische Studien*, 27 Band. Leipzig, 1900.]

INDEX